Pearl S. Buck's
Chinese Women Characters

Pearl S. Buck's
Chinese Women Characters

Xiongya Gao

Selinsgrove: Susquehanna University Press
London: Associated University Presses

Associated University Presses
440 Forsgate Drive
Cranbury, NJ 08512

Associated University Presses
16 Barter Street
London WC1A 2AH, England

Associated University Presses
P.O. Box 338, Port Credit
Mississauga, Ontario
Canada L5G 4L8

The paper used in this publication meets the requirements
of the American National Standard for Permanence of Paper
for Printed Library Materials Z39.48–1984.

Library of Congress Cataloging-in-Publication Data

Gao, Xiongya, 1955–
    Pearl S. Buck's Chinese women characters / Xiongya Gao.
        p. cm.
    Includes bibliographical references and index.
    ISBN 1-57591-025-X (alk, paper)
    1. Buck, Pearl S. (Pearl Sydenstricker), 1892–1973—Knowledge—China. 2. Buck, Pearl S. (Pearl Sydenstricker), 1892–1973—Characters—Women. 3. Women and literature—United States—History—20th century. 4. Women and literature—China—History—20th century. 5. American fiction—Chinese influences. 6. China—In literature. 7. Women in literature. I. Title.

PS3503.U198 Z68 2000
813'.52—dc21   99-086340

PRINTED IN THE UNITED STATES OF AMERICA

Contents

Pearl S. Buck's
Chinese Women Characters

1

Introduction

Pᴇᴀʀʟ sʏᴅᴇɴsᴛʀɪᴄᴋᴇʀ ʙᴜᴄᴋ (1892–1973) ɪs ᴏɴᴇ ᴏғ ᴛʜᴇ ᴍᴏsᴛ ʀᴇɴᴏᴡɴᴇᴅ ᴀᴍᴇʀɪᴄᴀɴ writers. She enjoys both high acclaim and recognition from the literary community and great popularity from readers, especially during the thirties through the sixties. While her recognition and popularity testify to her literary achievements, they alone do not fully reveal her uniqueness as an American writer and her unparalleled contribution to world literature in general and American literature in particular. She was, most importantly, an author who existed "in one world and not of it, and belonging to another world and yet not of it" (Buck 1954, 51).

Although American-born (in Hillsboro, West Virginia) and American-educated (B.A., Randolph-Macon Woman's College, 1914; M.A., Cornell, 1926), Buck spent her childhood and adolescent years in China—from the age of four months to seventeen—and later lived and taught in China irregularly between 1910 and 1934, when she took up permanent residence in America. This firsthand experience enabled Buck in most of her works to "present to us China as the Chinese sees it, but in language (of both lip and mind) which we can understand" (Bentley 1935, 793), serving as a bridge between the East and the West.

In her mission to introduce, primarily through literature, the real China to Westerners, Buck was especially successful in presenting its people— among whom the women stood out most vividly. In her thirteen novels that have Chinese settings and Chinese main characters, Buck depicted a large range of Chinese women: from imperial women of the ruling class to servant women who are at the bottom of the society; from urban women to rural women; from old, traditional women to new, liberated, and educated women. This book will study the characterization in five of Buck's novels: *East Wind: West Wind* (1930), *The Good Earth* (1932b), *The Mother* (1934), *Pavilion of Women* (1946), and *Peony* (1948b), concentrating on the typicality and individuality of the characters in them. Among the most important novels by the author, and all having women as their main characters, these novels are representative of Buck's work and offer a wide array of women characters with different beliefs, personalities, and social and economic backgrounds.

I will examine to what degree Buck's women characters are typical of Chinese women in general and to what degree they are individualized figures, facing different conflicts, in a variety of social, familial situations, with their respective unique characteristics. It will be demonstrated that these characters, viewed as a group, are both typical and individualized. Within the group, however, they are typical and individualized to different degrees. In other words, if we posit a continuum, typicality at one end and individuality at the other, we find Buck's women characters fall on different points along this continuum. And the point on which a particular character falls is determined by the overall theme of the novel in question. For example, if one finds that character X is less individualized than Y, it is because the novel in which X appears calls for a less individualized character in order to aid its theme. Therefore, characterization will not be examined in isolation, but in relation to other aspects of the novels.

The following three classifications will be frequently referred to: stereotypical, typical, and individualized. I will define "stereotypical" as the images of the Chinese in the Western mind at that time, which are often distorted and derogatory. "Typical" will be taken in its dictionary sense, referring to a character who possesses characteristics common to the type to which she belongs. "Individualized" will be used to refer to characters who stand out from the typical and can be described as none other than themselves, characters who do things differently from those in the same type.

In presenting genuinely typical features of her characters, Buck provides her Western readers with a true picture of the Chinese people, thus destroying the stereotypical images Westerners have long had of the Chinese. This accomplishment, of course, grows out of Buck's lifelong effort to promote understanding among all peoples and her philosophy that we should tolerate one another and live in harmony. By giving her characters individuality, Buck makes her characters stand out vividly. Each character has her own features and traits and behaves in her own way. By skillfully combining typicality with individuality, Buck adds a series of Chinese women to the gallery of imperishable literary characters, placing herself among the greatest writers in the world.

There is a common characteristic among all major women characters in the novels examined in this book: they all make best use of their very limited power allowed by the society to achieve what they deserve. Their actions quite often appear calculating and manipulative. This is seen, as will become clear, not as a faulty personality trait, but as a result of the oppression that Chinese women have faced throughout their lives. In order to survive, they have to act in ways acceptable to society; but to achieve dignity, happiness, and freedom for themselves, they have also learned to use their intelligence to steer unfavorable situations to their advantage while still appearing to honor the traditions, the moral standards, and the virtues society imposes on them. As Wang Ma, a servant character in *Peony*, puts it: "Obey—obey—and do what you like. The two go together—if you are clever" (56). They take whatever life offers them and make the best use of it for the benefit of themselves as well as of those around them.

Buck the Writer

As a writer, Buck has had unprecedented recognition. She is the only woman recipient of both the Pulitzer Prize and the Nobel Prize for literature to date, and her works have been among the most widely translated in the history of American literature. Robert Spiller's *Literary History of the United States* (1948), for example, records that Buck's work "was particularly liked in Sweden. Ten of her books appeared there between 1932 and 1940, more than were translated from any other American author during the years covered by the *Index Translationuum*" (2:1383). In Denmark, she "was the most popular American author from 1932 to 1939 . . . but Hemingway and Steinbeck had succeeded her by 1940" (2:1384). Based on this and other information, the noted Buck scholar Paul Doyle writes, in *Pearl S. Buck*:

> What was generally true in Sweden and Denmark held for much of the world. Eventually, Pearl Buck's writings were translated into every important language in the world. She and Mark Twain have become unrivaled among American writers—both past and present—for their top-ranking place of popularity in countries overseas. (Doyle 1980, 81)

Furthermore, Buck's books were almost always widely reviewed in journals when they appeared, as if readers the world over were waiting for her products. *The Good Earth*, for example, drew twenty-three reviews in 1931, *Sons* twenty-one in 1932, *The Mother* twenty-four in 1934, and *The Exile* twenty-two in 1936 (Overton 1942, 30–33). These reviews, with a few exceptions to be discussed later, spoke highly of Buck's novels.

Mention should also be made about Buck's productivity. During her lifetime, she wrote some forty-six novels, two biographies of her mother and father, two autobiographies, numerous short stories and articles, and about eleven other full-length works of nonfiction. She also translated one of the most famous Chinese novels, *Shui Hu Zhuan* (All Men Are Brothers), into English.[1]

Buck's literary talent caused her name to be seen in print even when she was seven: On April 5, 1899, *The Christian Observer*, a newspaper published in Louisville, Kentucky, carried a letter to the editor signed Sydenstricker, Chinkiang (Zhenjiang), China. "This early success," she recalled years later, "made me willing, if not always eager, to follow my mother's suggestion again and begin writing regularly" (Harris 1969, 87). By the time she was ten, Buck was able to obtain regular pocket money through the prizes she got for writing the best stories and articles for a newspaper published under British auspices in Shanghai, China.

Despite all this, Buck's work has not been universally appreciated. First, although Buck was one of the most widely translated American writers, very few of her works have been published in Chinese in China's mainland. This is, at least partly, the reason that only a few critical works have appeared on Buck by Chinese critics—who are, arguably, better judges of her than their Western counterparts. Second, although Buck's works were considered to be "rich and genuine portrayals of Chinese peasant life" by the Nobel Prize in Literature Committee, she was accused by some former Chinese authorities of "an attitude of distortion, smear, and vilification towards the people of new China and their leaders" (Buck 1972, 172).

While the unfair treatment Buck received from the Chinese governments may be perplexing to Westerners, it is not difficult for a Chinese person to understand. For whatever motive, governments in China, both the Nationalists before 1949 and the Communists after 1949, have always wanted China's condition to be portrayed better than it actually was. The following instances recorded by Buck herself illustrate this well. When a European dignitary visited China in the 1920s, matting was set up on both sides of the street in certain sections of Nanjing so that the poor people and the slums would be hidden from his view (Buck 1954, 239). On another occasion, news accounts of the making of the movie *The Good Earth* in China revealed that the Chinese government would not allow people to appear in rags and bare feet for fear that this would give the Western world a "false" picture of Chinese life (393–94). The Chinese authorities also wanted the filmmakers to use a tractor instead of the traditional water buffalo, although at that time tractors were practically nonexistent in the country (394). When the Communists took over the mainland, they found themselves in a world largely hostile to the Communist movement. Therefore, they have, even to this day, tried to paint China as a much more "modernized" country than it is. For instance, in many Chinese movies, a typical family will live in a spacious, well-furnished apartment. In reality, however, the area of house per person is about eight square meters. They also use political rhetoric to hide negative sides of their society. For example, government reports seldom give figures of unemployment, creating an impression that there is no unemployment in China. The Chinese know, however, that the category the government has established, "youth waiting to be employed," refers to none other than the unemployed, and the number, although never officially revealed, remains alarming.

For a long time intellectuals could only write about what the government wanted them to write and in the way the government allowed. Being an American writing about Chinese life while residing in America freed Buck from these governmental controls, a fortunate fact for Buck and for the world. However, it has created an almost unprecedented literary tragedy, that one billion Chinese had long been barred from reading works about themselves by a writer who devoted most of her life to the faithful portrayal of them.

If Buck's readers find the treatment of Buck by the Chinese government unfair and inexcusable, they will be more mystified by Western critics' neglect of Buck as a major American writer. First, none of Buck's works seems to have been anthologized. Peter Conn, in his recent book, Pearl S. Buck: A Cultural Biography (1996), for example, admits:

> As recent as 1989, I published a 600-page history of American literature, in which I found room for everyone from the seventeenth-century Puritan preacher Urian Oakes to the twentieth-century proletarian propagandist Giacomo Patri, but I never mentioned Pearl S. Buck. (xii)

Also according to Conn, "In 1934, the year that Pearl Buck moved back to the United States, Malcolm Cowley published *Exiles Return*, his anecdotal history of the 'lost generation'." However, "Needless to say, neither Pearl's years in Asia nor her return to the United States was memorialized by Malcolm Cowley in his survey" (163).

Second, there have been only a small number of books, dissertations, and critical essays on Buck. Looking at Jeanne Overton's *Pearl Buck: Bibliography of Criticism*, published in 1942, one finds that the references to

Buck's works, everything included, occupy eighteen pages (8–25), while references to articles about Buck fill only a little more than three pages (26–29), totaling twenty-five entries. Further, among these twenty-five entries, most are biographical sketches, interviews with Buck, and news reports on Buck's receiving the Nobel Prize; only two are critical essays. Of course, Overton's bibliography is not a comprehensive bibliography and only records those works that appeared before 1942, but it gives us a glimpse of how Buck was ignored by serious critics at that time.[2] A thorough search has yielded only five books written about her, all either biographical or bibliographical, and only three dissertations are devoted to her literary works.

One anecdote is illustrative of how Buck was perceived by the critics. When news came that Buck was the recipient of Nobel Prize for literature in 1938, the American critical circle was surprised, and a few critics were even outraged (Doyle 1980, 81; Harris 1969, 257). Doyle records that

> It was claimed that she was too youthful, that she had written too few important books to be considered of major statue, and that no woman writer deserved the award. She was even charged with not being an American writer since her subject matter and even her places of residence were almost completely Chinese. (82)

Deeply depressed at this, Buck, when honored at a dinner in New York City, included in her speech an apologetic commentary on novel writing, regarding it as inferior to more scholarly composition like poetry and nonfiction prose.

The treatment, or rather mistreatment, of Buck by the critics is not only unfortunate for Buck as a writer, but also, when looked at in some depth, reveals some disheartening facts about the American literary tradition. First, Buck was neglected simply because "she was a women writer and especially, a woman Nobel Prize winner" (Doyle 1980, 8), writing primarily about women's lives, "a subject to which the men of the lost generation and their champions were collectively indifferent" (Conn 1996, 164). This illustrates a bias against women writers in general. Nina Baym (1981), for example, convincingly shows that as late as 1977, the canon of major writers did not include any women novelists (123), although "women authors have been active since the earliest days of settlement. Commercially and numerically they have probably dominated American literature since the middle of the nineteenth century" (124).

Similar facts have been recorded by other authors. According to Paul Lauter (1983), the National Council of Teachers of English in 1948 reviewed the study of American literature in college curricula and found that only three women writers appeared in the ninety syllabi of survey courses studied (439). In 1952, Ben W. Fuson, after surveying twenty-seven American literature anthologies, found that among the seventy authors whose works were substantially covered, only six women were represented.

Buck was, of course, very aware of how women writers were viewed. From the 1940s to the 1950s, when she decided to write about American subject matter, she used a pseudonym, John Sedges: "a simple one, and masculine because men have fewer handicaps in our society than women have in writing as well as in other professions" (Buck 1958, viii).[3] On another occasion, she remarked that "[W]omen artists in any field are not taken as seriously as men, however serious their work. It is true that they often achieve high popular success. But this counts against them as artists" (Buck 1941, 67).

The second factor contributing to the neglect of Buck by critics is that her works deal with "Chinese and Asiatic materials" (Doyle 1980, 8). As Baym (1981) succinctly demonstrates, American literary criticism has long been dominated by a "nationalistic orientation." As a result, literary excellence has been synonymous with being American (125–26). Works of subject matter other than American are of secondary interest at best.

There may be a third reason for Buck's neglect: fear on the part of critics. This is due to the multicultural nature of Buck's best works, according to Jane M. Rabb, who wrote the entry on Buck for *Notable American Women*. Buck's work requires much from her critics: familiarity with cultural environments often considered foreign and exotic, a knowledge of Buck's private life (which is unusually complex), and an understanding of "the traditional Chinese novel, the King James Bible, and classic American and English fiction of the last two centuries as well as the models in other literary genres she [Buck] utilized" (Rabb 1992, 7). Rabb seems to imply that, not equipped with all these prerequisites, critics have simply ignored and discounted Buck as a major writer.[4]

However, I would like to end this section on a happier note: There seems, recently, to have been a renewed interest in Buck in the United States. Most of Buck's major novels, including the five studied in this book, have been reprinted in paperback. In March 1992, the Pearl S. Buck Centennial Symposium was held at Randolph-Macon Woman's College, with participants from China as well as the United States. The proceedings, edited by Elizabeth J. Lipscomb, Frances E. Webb, and Peter Conn, were published in 1994. In June 1993, WSWP/Beckley and Refocus Films released on public television a film, "East Wind, West Wind: Pearl S. Buck, The Woman Who

Embraced the World," which follows Buck's life, with a historical perspective provided by some of the world's well-known scholars on China, such as the late John K. Fairbank of Harvard University and James C. Thomson of Boston University. In 1996, Peter Conn published his *Pearl S. Buck: A Cultural Biography* as an "effort to reclaim Buck's life and work" (xviii).

Meanwhile, in the People's Republic of China, where Buck's works were banned for decades, scholars have begun to pay attention to Buck and her works. In 1988, Buck's *Good Earth* trilogy, *The House of Earth: The Good Earth, Sons,* and *A House Divided*, was translated and published in the People's Republic of China for the first time since 1949. In January 1991, the first Pearl S. Buck Conference was held in Zhenjiang, Buck's Chinese hometown. In July 1997, Buck and her works were a major interest at the International Symposium on Chinese-American Cultural Interactions: 1840–1949, held in Nanjing University. At both conferences, Buck reclaimed her reputation among Chinese scholars, who acknowledged her contribution in introducing China and her people to the West, rectifying the distorted images of the Chinese in the mind of Westerners.

Buck's Critics

Just as most of Buck's works are about Chinese life, most of the critical literature on Buck is about how various aspects of the Chinese life are faithfully and realistically portrayed and how these works are related to Chinese society.

First of all, critics seem to agree that Buck's works about Chinese life are generally more appealing than her works on American life. Commenting on Buck's novels, for example, Yuh-chao Yu (1988) points out: "The fact remains that the general response to her 'American novels' has been far less enthusiastic or favorable than her 'Asian novels.'" Yu attributes this to Buck's knowing Asia, especially China, "much more intimately than America" (23). In his book, Doyle speaks highly of Buck's Chinese novels, like *The Good Earth, The Mother*, and *The Patriot*. However, he apparently thinks much less of Buck's American novels. He comments that among the five novels published under the pseudonym John Sedges, only one of them, *The Townsman*, "is of especial importance" (Doyle 1980, 113). None of Buck's other works with Western subject matter, Doyle seems to maintain, is successful. These works include *Command the Morning*, a story of the Manhattan Project, with too heavy a touch of propaganda and didacticism and a failure in characterization (127), and *A Desert Incident*, about scientists working on a secret governmental project at a site in the Arizona desert, in which "Buck's venture into symbolism is disastrous" (128).

A situation parallel to this is found in Buck's short stories. In her review of Buck's fourteen stories, M. M. Bitker (1961) writes that "[a]lthough the stories with American background are as skillfully wrought and their points are aptly made, they have not the impact of novelty" (41).

Critics also generally agree that Buck's works about Chinese life are faithful and realistic (but see below for an exception). This view reflects the Western critics' (as well as the general public's) confidence in Buck's knowledge of Chinese life—a confidence that is present, either overtly or covertly, in almost all the reviews of Buck and in the biographies and critical articles on Buck's works. Theodore F. Harris (1969), for instance, records that at a press conference, a newsman asked:

> Pearl Buck undoubtedly knows more about China and the Chinese people, more about Asia and Asian people, cultures and governments than any other American and possibly more than any other person alive. Why is it that we do not ask at least her opinion of or her advice on our current Asian policies? (269)

The faithfulness of Buck's portrayal of Chinese life seems to be a recurrent comment in many of the reviews of her novels. For example, *The Mother*'s appearance on the bookstore shelf in 1934 was accompanied by a one-and-one-half page review in the *New York Times*, entitled "A True Epitome of Motherhood" (Adams 1934). The reviewer painstakingly examines the details of the mother's life in the novel, showing that Buck's representation of this Chinese woman's life is truthful and credible.

However, criticisms that came from Chinese scholars were much less favorable. In fact, they bluntly accused Buck of having presented an untrue picture of Chinese life to the West. After *The Good Earth* was published in 1931, two Asian critics, Younghill Kang (1931), a Korean writer, and Kang-hu Kiang (1933), a Chinese scholar, argued that Buck's portrayal of Chinese life was highly distorted. The following is the gist of Kiang's criticisms, to which Kang's is extremely similar.

First, Kiang openly discredited Western writers' works on Chinese life: "I must admit that I never cared much to read Western writers on Chinese subjects and still less their novels about China." Because many of his friends repeatedly inquired of him about Buck's works, he "picked up *The Good Earth* and glanced over it in one evening." He "felt uneasy at her minute descriptions of certain peculiarities and defects of some lowly bred Chinese characters." These characters were, though not entirely untrue, "very uncommon" in the Chinese life he knew (1).

Besides, Kiang found fault with many of Buck's details. He denied as "untrue and unheard of" the notion that the Chinese would send for priests to call a woman's soul back to life after her suicide (an incident in *East Wind: West Wind*). To him, no Chinese would drop the *Book of Changes*, a sacred and holy book always treated with reverence and respect, on the floor as Buck's character does. He also remarked that cows would not be killed and eaten in China, that tea is always made in China by pouring hot water over the tea leaves rather than by sprinkling leaves upon the surface of the water as Buck described in *The Good Earth*, and that Chinese medicine never included tiger's heart and dog's tooth. Therefore, Kiang concluded, Buck did not know China well enough to write accurately about her people, although she had been reared there.

Fortunately for Buck, however, the *New York Times* allowed her to reply to Kiang's essay in the same issue. She rebutted Kiang's attacks both in general and point by point. She wrote that she was "present when the young woman was cut down from the beam where she had hung herself." Then "priests were called in at once, in the hope of restoring her soul to her still warm body" (Buck 1933a, 2). She had also seen with her own eyes a woman drop *The Book of Changes* to the floor, although she knew that theoretically the sacred book should not be thus treated. She had firsthand knowledge that in many parts of China cows were frequently killed, and she had received the tiger's heart and dog's tooth prescription in a medicine shop. In the region she used as the locale for *The Good Earth*, "a few tea leaves are sprinkled upon the surface of hot water, where tea is scarce" (2).

As a native Chinese, I can also testify, with knowledge from my own experience, that these details Kiang claimed to be false are in fact true. In the northwestern part of the country where I was born and reared, peasants do, even to this day, send for priests to call back the soul of a dying person. I also know for a fact that northerners in China kill cows and eat beef.

Those Chinese critics' attacks, like those of Kiang, reveal a gulf between intellectuals and ordinary people in China. Buck herself, for example, pointed out that she was very familiar with Kiang's attitude that China should be represented to the Western world by its scholars and intellectuals rather than by its peasants and common people. She very much regretted that some of China's intellectuals tend to be ashamed of the common people and to ignore their existence, while they should be proud of them because they are "China's strength and glory." About this somewhat perplexing phenomenon, Doyle (1980) summarizes well when he writes the following:

> In the long history of China a gap has always existed between the Chinese intellectuals and the ordinary men and women who make up the bulk of the population. In general, these intellectuals not only look down upon the common man, but they do not even know the common man. Many of these scholars have been educated at foreign universities, and this training and background often drives them further away from the peasant classes. (45)

To this, I might add a somewhat harsher remark: For those intellectuals who do know the common man, they tend to think that he is backward, shameful, and even uncivilized. As a result, they think that they are the real representatives of China while the common man's existence ought to be forgotten. As recorded by Buck (1954), when some Chinese students in New York City were giving Buck a dinner, they asked her not to publish her translation of *Shui Hu Zhuan* (All Men Are Brothers) because the story contained a cannibal scene that they felt would give Western readers a disrespectful view of Chinese life (282–83).

The Chinese critics' attacks have done considerable damage to Buck's reputation. "Even to this day," Doyle notes, "the suspicion exists in certain American critical quarters that Buck has not portrayed Chinese peasant life with accuracy" (46).

On the other hand, however, seldom have Buck's works been treated as works of art. The numerous reviews of her work, for example, are disappointing in this respect because, when they talk about the artistry of Buck (in fact, very few do), they tend to use vague and general terms without detailed explanation of what they actually mean. When reviewing *East Wind: West Wind*, for instance, Edwin Seaver (1930) uses words such as "a very good novel," "a fine simplicity and delicacy and charm," and "an exquisite book" (10m); *Book-of-the-Month Club News* (quoted in Harris 1969, 194) says, about *The Good Earth*, that "Mrs. Buck has the story teller's gift. She sees life like a reel unfolding, scene after scene, each exhibiting characters"; and J. Donald Adams (1934) praises *The Mother* as "a true epitome of motherhood" and "a unity and a driving simplicity and strength to a degree more marked than in any of Mrs. Buck's previous work" (1).

Dorothy Canfield's (1932) review of *Sons* speaks more highly of this novel than any other. However, we see again that the descriptive words she uses are empty, without supporting discussion:

The characters are much more sharply individualized in *Sons* than in *The Good Earth* or perhaps they are merely mounded out. . . . There is more power in the new book, and a wider scope. The power is diffused: the structure less compact. Yet it is captious to pick flaws in a book which has so much that is extraordinarily fine in it. The prose is superb, full of music and simple dignity.

In a sense, reviews are not supposed to provide scrutiny of the artistic successes or failures of the work under review. But if we exclude reviews from our consideration when looking for criticisms of Buck's artistry, there is simply not much to be found. The following are the opinions of the few who have commented on Buck's literary achievements.

The first notable element in Buck's literary artistry is her style. Critics have used descriptions like "simplicity" (Doyle 1980, 33), "biblical," and "King James Version" (Carson 1939, 56, among others) to indicate her stylistic characteristics. Buck's language, Bentley (1935) says, "is English— very plain English: yet it gave the impression that one is reading the language native to the characters all the time." He points out further: "The grave, biblical speech, full of dignity, in which Mrs. Buck, without ever 'raising her voice', is able to render both the deepest and the lightest emotions—the feeling of a mother over her dead child and the excitement of an old man over his tea—is a fine example of an instrument perfectly adapted to its task" (793).

However, as some critics have noted, this simplicity can fail the author, becoming oversimplicity and monotonousness. Doyle (1980), for example, points out that the prose of *The Mother* "is reduced to the barest simplicity. It is less rich, poetic and varied. . . ." This leads Doyle to the conclusion that the biblical–Chinese saga style "can be drawn too thin or be too simple in a lengthy narrative and, hence, lacks a vital heightening and variety of tone and harmony" (65).

Doyle also notes that while the simplicity of style has proven effective in Buck's farm or rural descriptions, it loses its picturesqueness in, and becomes out of harmony with, the portrayal of a more modern, dynamic mode of existence, such as the rendering of life in big cities like Shanghai and Nanjing and scenes in the United States in *A House Divided*. This view is also shared by other critics, such as Bentley.

Critics seem to have agreed that characterization is another strength of Buck, particularly her success in creating a wide range of characters— characters of every age, sex, class, and type. This achievement, Bentley

(1935) believes, primarily results from the writer's objectivity in the presentation of characters. "She does not color her characters too much with her own feelings about them, but always allows them to be just and righteous, even though she disapproves of them, and a little peevish and weak, even though they be her heroes" (795). As a result, most of Buck's main characters are individualized, which in fact is an important mark of literary success.

The individuality of Buck's characters has had a strong universal appeal to readers. English-speaking readers find themselves able to relate to Buck's characters even though these characters belong to a people foreign to them. James Gray (1946), for example, compliments Buck on her enabling Western readers to know China with "sanity, compassion and understanding" (33). Adams (1944) asserts that *The Good Earth* makes "America aware, in the lives of a completely alien people, of universal human bonds" (125). According to Carl Van Doren (1940), "*The Good Earth* for the first time made the Chinese seem as familiar as neighbors" (353) in the United States. Further, E. H. A. Carson (1939) writes that:

> The central character in *The Mother* with little change might be typical of a sharecropper family in the southern States as of a peasant family in central China. Much of *The Good Earth* might well be reenacted with little change in lines by a family flooded out of the Mississippi flats and forced to migrate to California. (56)

About *The Mother*, Henchoz (1943) says the following:

> In fact, Pearl Buck does not give a proper name to this mother, she is anonymous, for she has all the qualities of a mother, no matter to what race she belongs. Renunciation, self-sacrifice and absence of vanity—we find all these virtues in various degrees in our own parents. (98)

Looking at Buck's work as a whole, we find that the individuality and universality of characters play an important part, if not the most important part, in her literary success.

Among these critical works on Buck hitherto reviewed, which have concentrated on the writer's style and characterization, Bentley is the only writer who comments on other aspects of Buck's literary skills. First, Bentley (1935) observes that in terms of scene, Buck attempts to "present China from within, as the Chinese see it." For example, the landscape in Buck's novels is always presented as seen by familiar eyes: "The dawns are lurid with beauty to the stranger, where the native sees the coming rain or the rising of the wind" (792). Similarly, when describing Chinese customs, Buck never calls her readers' attention to the difference of these customs from the their own.

In terms of plot, Bentley points out, first, that Buck's novels have all the incidents "that might happen in man or woman's life—death, birth, marriage; love, hate, jealousy; fear, famine and flood; repine and slaughter; peaceful family life; battles and revolution; tragedy, comedy; the most exquisite tenderness and the vilest cruelty." All these incidents are handled in "the epic rather than the dramatic form." Her stories are chronological, with few, if any, flashbacks. There is always one point of view, "straightforward, without devices." The plot is never complex, belonging to the "single-strand type" (798).

Finally, Bentley maintains that the theme of Buck's works is not so much her intention to present China to the West, neither is it her aim to present the transition from the old China to the new, although both might be true to some extent, as it is her desire to present "The continuity of life" (798–99). To Bentley, the anonymous mother, the man, the old woman, the girl, the townsman, and the younger boy in *The Mother* are, respectively, "all mothers, all townsmen, all old women, all brothers and sisters; what they say and do is deeply true to all human motive, so that we sympathize and understand." Therefore, "to read her novels is to gain not merely knowledge of China but wisdom of life" (800).

About the Chinese women characters in Buck, there are, besides some sporadic allusions by critics in their criticisms on other facets of Buck's works, two somewhat detailed treatments. The first one is a chapter by Caoly Doan in his dissertation on the image of the Chinese family in Buck's novels (1965), and the second is an M.A. thesis by Li Bo in 1989, which deals with how Chinese characters, both male and female, are portrayed by several American writers, including Buck.

Doan's chapter examines women characters in seven of Buck's novels: *Pavilion of Women, Kinfolk, East Wind: West Wind, The Good Earth, Dragon Seed, Peony,* and *The Mother.* He finds that, generally, "Pearl Buck's Chinese women possess better qualities than her Chinese men" (103). If the women are "members of an aristocratic family they never share the sham which characterizes their men" (104). The reason for this, Doan says, is that Buck, as a woman, understands Chinese women better than Chinese men (118).

This view is shared by others. Peter Conn (1996) holds that "Buck's fiction broke new ground in subject matter, especially in her representations of Asia, and above all in her portraits of Asian women" (xiii). Carson (1939) writes that it is her portrayal of women that "places Pearl Buck among the first of the really creative novelists" (59).

Comparing Buck's Chinese characters with those in Mark Twain, John Steinbeck, Bret Harte, and Frank Norris, Li (1989) finds that the latter writers, all white males, "did not help understand the Chinese better, but, on the contrary, contributed in different degrees to the misconceptions and stereotypes in Western minds" (118). Buck is the only American writer "whose writings about the Chinese were not misleading and helped considerably in erasing misunderstanding from Western minds" (110).

These two studies, however, appear limited in both scope and depth. Doan's chapter does not seem to be more than a shallow treatment of the subject. For instance, he does not examine women's position in society; neither does he link Buck's characterization of Chinese women to other aspects of her work. Li's thesis seems even more superficial than Doan's chapter: The conclusion that Buck's portrayal of Chinese women is faithful and realistic says something that critics had being saying for decades.

Buck's Chinese Influence

Having been reared and having lived in China, Buck was undoubtedly influenced by that nation and its people. These influences made themselves felt in Buck's works and in her view about life and the world. To understand Buck well, therefore, one cannot ignore her Chinese influence.

Buck was born to Absalom and Caroline Sydenstricker on 26 June 1892, in Hillsboro, West Virginia. Only four months after her birth, her missionary parents took her to China. Her entire childhood was spent in that country; she resided in a bungalow in Zhenjiang, a port city on the Yangtze River, until she was seventeen (with a brief visit to her birthplace at the age of ten).

As she recalled later, this period in her life played an important role in making her what she was to become later (Harris 1969, 31–50). In these early, formative years, "China stamped itself indelibly on the young child's mind and imagination" (Doyle 1980, 16). During this time, she learned Chinese as her first language, mingled with Chinese children in the neighborhood, and listened to Chinese stories. She later admits that she was "a curious child plaguing everyone with questions sometimes too intimate and personal" (Buck 1954, 62).

Her Chinese nurse, Wang Amah, provided her with endless stories, especially Buddhist and Taoist legends, which she considered to be the first literary influence she received (Buck 1932c). The life stories of this nurse also remained in her mind all her life (Harris 1969). She told her biographer, Theodore Harris, that Wang Amah "is one of the two clear figures in the dimness of my early childhood. Foremost stands my mother, but close beside her, sometimes almost seeming a part of her, I see, when I look back, the blue-coated figure of my old Chinese nurse" (31).

It is also during this time that she received her Chinese education from her tutor, Mr. Kung. For a number of years, he taught her not only Chinese reading and writing but also Confucian ethics and Chinese history. He also made her alert to Western imperialism and exploitation in the Far East (Doyle 1980, 18). When he died in 1905, Buck felt a great sorrow and acknowledged that she learned from him "the first axiom of human life," that is, "Every event has had its cause, and nothing, not the least wind that blows, is accident or causeless" (Buck 1954, 58). Yu (1988) believes that it is under Mr. Kung's tutelage that Buck's "knowledge of Chinese culture began to take root" (25).

Buck's Chinese education and influence undoubtedly played their part in her early success in literature at Randolph-Macon Woman's College where she completed her B.A. degree during 1910–1914. There she wrote stories for the college monthly and other campus publications, collaborated on a class play, and won two literary prizes in her senior year, one for the best short story contest and the other for the best poem (Doyle 1980, 19).

Three years after Buck returned to China in 1914, she married John Lossing Buck, an American agricultural expert. The couple went to live in Nanxuzhou, Anhui province, in Northern China. There she became intimately acquainted with the ways of Chinese peasants, their farming methods, their struggles with drought and famine, and the ordinary day-to-day activities of their existence. During the frequent trips with her husband to the countryside, she would converse with women and children and observe their life. She became fascinated with the farming families who worked incredibly hard but had very little to show for it. For Buck, these farming people of North China "were the most real, the closest to the earth, to birth and death, to laughter and to weeping. To visit the farm families became my own search of reality, and among them I found human being as he most really is" (Buck 1954, 146). "From this time on there deepened in her a pervading and abiding love of the Chinese peasant, a love which infused her whole being and carried over into her literary works" (Doyle 1980, 21).

After living for five years in North China, Buck and her husband moved to Nanjing where she taught English literature at three different universities for the next ten years before she took permanent residence in the United States. In Nanjing, however, she experienced a completely different China, a China in transition, if not in political and ideological turmoil. Western ideas were beginning to infiltrate and challenge old traditional Chinese customs. Many young Chinese were in ferment and rebellion. The university students, who had been reared in a conservative and patriarchal family system, were especially confused and bewildered at new liberal ideas and modes of thought. Being trapped between the old and the new, many of them looked to Western countries for enlightenment and solution to their problems, only to find inconsistences and corruption in Western idealism (Doyle 1980, 21).

Being able to see both the rural Chinese life and the urban is a rare experience for even a Chinese, let alone an American. This experience offered Buck the material and the insight for many of her major works, including *The Good Earth*, *A House Divided*, *Sons*, and *East Wind: West Wind*.

China and her people left a strong mark on Buck both as a writer and as a person. As a writer, she adopted the goal of the Chinese novelists in novel writing. In her Nobel lecture (1939), she discussed the influence Chinese novels had on her. After an analysis of the development of the Chinese novel, she said: "In this tradition of the novel have I been born and reared as a writer. My ambition, therefore, has not been trained toward the beauty of letters or the grace of art" (55). What is her goal in novel writing, then? She accepted the doctrine of most Chinese novelists, who place great emphasis on portraying the life of the people, convinced that the realities of human life are the most important subject for novelists, and that the fundamental measure of a novel is whether the characters are alive. To summarize, she declared: "No, a novelist must not think of pure literature as his goal. . . . He must be satisfied if the common people hear him gladly. At least, so I have been taught in China" (59). Therefore, she did not write novels for their own sake, but for moral, spiritual, and perhaps societal purposes.

What is an artistic portrayal of the life of the people? For example, should the fictional characters in a novel be real people? The answer to this question can be found in her alumnae address, "On the Writing of Novels," delivered at Randolph-Macon Woman's College in June 1933. She told her audience that characters in her work are both more simple and more complex than ordinary human beings. They are simple because they are turned into fictional figures so that they will fit the atmosphere, theme, and total picture. Anything that does not agree with the overall features of the scene and the story must be suppressed. They are more complex because to them the novelist adds her own touches and flourishes.

To carry out the goal of portraying the life of the people, Buck believes that the novelist should abide by the *tse ran* principle. She said:

> A good novelist, so I have been taught in China, should be above all else *tse ran*, that is, natural, unaffected, and so flexible and variable as to be wholly at the command of the material that flows through him. His whole duty is only to sort life as it flows through him, and in the vast fragmentariness of time and space and event to discover essential and inherent order and rhythm and shape. (Buck 1939, 31)

Based on the *tse ran* principle, Buck achieved several qualities in her work. First, she treated characterization as the most crucial element in novel writing (Doyle 1980, 84). Like the Chinese author, she preferred to use an omniscient point of view and chose to portray the characters more by presenting their behaviors and dialogues than by describing the states of their minds. Their motivations are usually explained, but only to the extent that the story can be carried on smoothly (Yu 1988, 34).

Second, Buck held that loose coordination in plot structure is not necessarily a defect. She noted (1932a) that, unlike the English novel, the Chinese novel does not seem to have a strictly planned beginning and ending. "There is no climax, nor denouement. There is often not even a main plot, except as one may call the events which circle about the main character, if there is a main character, a plot. There is no formal subordination of subplot" (10). This structural feature is, in fact, a virtue: It "may be a technique, which if not deliberately planned, is yet unconsciously modeled after the incoherence of life itself" (38).

Third, Buck did not believe that one method or style is intrinsically better than another. The artist should choose the most appropriate form for her material. She asserted that the novelist who is interested more in form than in people is not creative, but only inventive. "If the writer is obsessed with the story and the characters, then the story and characters develop the most suitable form for their revelation" (Doyle 1980, 85).

Fourth, Buck maintained that although the genuine artist should not be a preacher, didacticism is acceptable so long as the novel portrays life faithfully and forcefully, for life itself is a good teacher. She stated (1933b):

Art, then, can be didactic, perhaps even purposefully so, if it portrays life whole and steadfastly. But it takes the highest genius to use didacticism. And highest genius never so uses it, for highest genius has always that strong cosmic awareness which prevents obsession with a theory and preserves proportion, that proportion which is an essential to art. (9)

The Chinese influence on Buck as a writer can help explain her strengths and weaknesses. On the one hand, she has been praised by many as a gifted storyteller and was considered to be skillful in characterization. On the other, we see in her work no stream-of-consciousness technique as in Joyce, no dexterous use of symbolism as in Hawthorne and Gordimer, no detailed psychoanalysis as in Henry James, no well-designed plot structure as in Flaubert, and no variety of point of view as in Faulkner and Conrad.

Buck was equally influenced by the Chinese as a person and as a writer. Having lived in China and America, she found that "It would be hard for me to declare which side of the world is most my own. . . . I am loyal to Asia as I am loyal to my own land" (Buck and Romulo 1958, 126). Less than a year before she died, she lovingly called China "my other country" (Doyle 1980, 15).

However, she was fully aware that she was not living in two worlds in perfect harmony. She knew both countries, loved both, but belonged to neither. Although two worlds met, interacted and mixed in her, she frequently found herself in between rather than having both. She sensed this even when a very young child. Harris, her biographer (1969), comments on her early childhood, for example: "She loves her birth country of America, but her first knowledge of her own land is of ways strange and foreign to her. She loved her mother's stories about the stately old house in the hills of West Virginia, and of the people there, but these too were foreign to her" (43). She had always identified herself as Chinese until one day she was called a "foreign devil" (Yu 1988, 24). After the Boxer Uprising in 1900, she discovered that:

My worlds no longer interwove. They were sharply clear, one from the other. I was American, not Chinese, and although China was as dear to me as my native land, I knew it was not my land. Mine was the country across the sea, the land of my forefathers, alien to China and indifferent to the Chinese people. (Buck 1954, 55)

Just as the people in China viewed the white girl as different and foreign, her American peers at Randolph-Macon Woman's College did not treat her as an in-group member when she first arrived there. She had to deliberately dress and speak in a more Western manner so as to feel at ease, only to find that her efforts came to no avail (Doyle 1980; Yu 1988).

The year 1927 saw one of the most dramatic events in Buck's life when an antiforeign movement erupted in Nanjing. She made a narrow escape because some Chinese friends offered to hide her from the attacking army. She wrote later about that escape:

> I have had that strong and terrible experience of facing death because of my color. At that time nothing I might have done could have saved me. I could not hide my race. The only reason I was not killed was because some of those in that other race knew me, under my skin, and risked their own lives for me and mine. (Quoted in Yu 1988, 24)

She understood that while the antiforeign sentiment of the Chinese at the time was not justifiable in its entirety, it was undoubtedly a result of the Western imperialists' exploitation of that country. Therefore, this and other incidents did not arouse any hatred in her toward the Chinese. Instead, they made her aware of the importance of mutual understanding among peoples of all colors. As Yu points out, "This realization helps to explain her lifelong preoccupation with her self-imposed task of promoting racial equality and improving cross-cultural communication for the sake of world-peace" (1988, 25).

When talking about Buck's Chinese background, one should not forget the fact that she was a native-born American, educated in America, and lived in her home country from 1934 till her death in 1973. Her intercultural experience made her "mentally bifocal" (Buck 1954, 57). "As a consequence, she had gained a uniquely cosmopolitan perspective, which equipped her to make valuable comparisons between Eastern and Western cultures" (Conn 1996, 163). She saw the strong points of both the American and the Chinese and their respective weaknesses. She saw the injustice the Westerners had done to the Chinese as well as the negatives, caprices, and petulance among those Chinese who were prone to blame all their troubles on their former masters and to shirk their own responsibility for improving their lot and developing their own leadership (Doyle 1980, 133). She saw similarities as well as differences between the Western culture and the oriental culture. For instance, she supposed that "Confucius was the same as Our Father in Heaven, that is, God the Father" and considered the Virgin Mary to be the "younger sister" of her favorite Goddess of Mercy, the Kwanyin (Buck 1954, 52).

However, experience and acculturation alone do not shape an individual. They only exert their influences on the personality traits, and innate qualities are perhaps stronger factors that make the individual the way she is. Buck's most important qualities, as Harris notes, are that she was always searching for the internal why and that she was detached from the people, although she was much involved with life and world affairs. Because, as a young child, Buck lived "in the dim world of in-between, she retreated into her own world and began to watch the passing parade of people as though from afar" (81). Harris records the following specific instance to illustrate this. When Buck was three years old, she was forced at times to stay within the compound. The gate was so near the ground that, try though she did, she could see no more of people than from the knees down. She was deeply interested, but detached behind the safety of the garden gate (81). She retained this aloofness all her life, which offered her an unique insight, both literally and figuratively, into the people around her, who went into her novels as composing elements of her characters.

Lastly, Buck's Chinese experience, together with her experience in her home country, made her a humanitarian in her later years (Doyle 1980). Having seen racial prejudice in both the Chinese and the American, she denounced it whenever she had a chance and "stressed the idea of humanity above all other concerns" (132). She believed that in a spirit of free inquiry and increased knowledge, American and Asia could come to know and understand each other's positions and improve their relations. Thus, as a writer, she sought in much of her work to explain Asians to Americans and Americans to Asians so as to bring about a mutual understanding of attitudes, differences, and problems. To Americans, she attempted in several of her works to explain why they were not popular in Asia, helping them to erase the "we-send-them-millions-of-dollars-in-aid-why-don't-they-like-us school of thought" (133). She also pointed out to Asians that they should not blame Westerners for all their suffering and problems. They had the responsibility to build their own countries.

2
Women in Chinese Society

Confucius's Doctrines

As THE MOST INFLUENTIAL SCHOOL OF THOUGHT IN CHINA AND ONE OF THE MOST influential in the Orient, Confucianism was held as the dominant social ideology by almost every feudal dynasty from approximately 200 B.C.E. to 1911 (when the Qing Dynasty was toppled), and by the nationalist government, which ruled the country from 1911 to 1949. As such, it has been the chief codifier of women's behavior in China.

However, the prejudice against women had existed in China long before Confucianism. According to Yutang Lin (1935), a famous Chinese scholar: "The fundamental dualistic outlook, with the differentiation of the *Yang* (male) and the *Yin* (female) principles, went back to the *Book of Changes*, which was later formulated by Confucius" (137).

A famous traditional Chinese cosmology, *Book of Changes* divides the world into two complementary elements: the *yin* and the *yang*. *Yin* refers to the feminine or negative principle in nature while *yang* refers to the masculine or positive principle. In the Chinese language, the *yin*, literally meaning "overcast" or "shade," is often used to refer to the female, symbolized by the moon, standing for all things dark, secret, hidden, cold, weak, and passive; and the *yang*, literally meaning "the sun" and figuratively referring to the male, standing for all things bright, open, overt, warm, strong, and active. *Yin Jian* is the world of the dead while *Yang Jie* is the world of the living. This sexual inequality is vividly illustrated in a song from the *Book of Poems* (approximately 200 B.C.E.):

> When a baby boy was born, he was laid on the bed, and given jade to play with, and when a baby girl was born, she was laid on the floor and given a tile to play with. (Quoted in Lin 1935, 137)

However, it was at the coming of Confucianism that the marriage system became the severe bondage of women and that the cult of feminine chastity became an obsession with men (Lin 1935, 138).

Confucius, like many other great ancient sages, did not leave behind him many books for his descendants, but only a collection of his teaching and dialogue with his students: *Lun Yu*, compiled by his students. In this relatively short collection, however, Confucius touches almost every aspect of life, teaching the Chinese how to behave in any conceivable situation. About women, however, he says very little:

> It is not pleasing to have to do with women or people of base condition. If you show them too much affection, they become too excited, and if you keep them at a distance, they are full of resentment. (Chap. 17)

From this, one sees the following: first, women are compared to people of "base condition": "inferior men," in other words. Second, women are unable to communicate and to understand. Third, as this is the only quote in Lun *Yu* about women, Confucius seems to suggest that women are to be forgotten, ignored, and passed over in silence.

However, women are half the human race after all, and they cannot totally be passed over in silence if men do not control them effectively. Therefore, based on the above quote, Confucius's followers developed a series of ceremonial "rites" for women. For example, in the *Book of Rites*, which contains rituals for all kinds of occasions in a strictly classified feudal society, married sisters could not eat at the same table with their brothers. These rites encourage and teach feminine virtues desirable from the male point of view, such as quietness, obedience, good manners, personal neatness, industry, ability to cook, to spin, and to sew, respect for the husband's parents, kindness to the husband's brothers, and courtesy to the husband's friends.

During the Han Dynasty (206 B.C.E.–219 C.E.), typical feminine virtues, namely obedience and loyalty, were developed into something like "feminine ethics," as Lin puts it. The most famous, or infamous, of these codes are the Three Obediences and Four Virtues *(San Cong Si De)*. The Three Obediences require women to obey the father before the marriage, obey the husband after marriage, and obey the first son after the death of husband. The Four Virtues are (sexual) morality, proper speech, modest manner, and diligent work. Pan Zhao, daughter of a famous literati and a loyal disciple of Confucius, was a great exponent of the Three Obediences and Four Virtues. In her book entitled *Precepts for Women (Nuijie)*, she exalted the submission and self-effacement of women before the authority of father and husband:

> In truth, as far as knowledge goes, a woman need not be extraordinarily intelligent. As for her speech, it need not be terribly clever. As for her appearance, it need not be beautiful or elegant; and for her talents, they need only be average. . . . This is why the Nuixian says "If a wife is like a shadow or an echo, how can you fail to praise her?" (Quoted in Kristeva 1974, 86)

The insistence on the inferiority of women could also be found in *The Book of Han Dynasty (Han Shu)*:

> When a newborn baby comes to the world, if it is a boy as strong as a wolf, his parents are still afraid that he might be too weak; whereas if it is a girl as sweet and as gentle as a little mouse, her parents still fear she might be too strong. (Quoted in Kristeva 1974, 76)

Consequently, women had no place at all in society. Yang Chen, a famous Confucianist of the time, even theorized it thus:

> If women are given work that requires contact with the outside, they will sow disorder and confusion throughout the Empire. Shame and injury will come to the Imperial Court, and the Sun and the Moon [Emperor and Empress] will wither away. The Book of Documents warns us against the hen who announces the dawn in place of the rooster; the Book of Odes denounces a clever women who overthrows a State . . . Women must not be allowed to participate in the affairs of government. (Quoted in Van Gulik 1971, 121)

As women's place was confined to home, loyalty of women to their husbands was cherished to such extent that a woman who died for her chastity would be officially honored with a plaque erected in a public place or with a title from the court, although women in this dynasty could still marry when their husbands died.

The morality imposed on women became even tighter in the Song Dynasty (420–478), when the remarrying of widows was made a moral crime by Confucian scholars. Lin (1935) observed that:

> Worship of chastity, which they so highly prized in women, became something of a psychological obsession, and women were henceforth to be responsible for social morals, from which the men were exempt. More than that, women were to be responsible for courage and strength of character

also, which curiously the men so admired in the gentle sex, for the emphasis had shifted from women's ordinary routine domestic virtues to female heroism and self-sacrifice. (141)

A woman who chose to end her life after her husband's death was held in high esteem and was greatly honored. The story that a widow cut off her arm because a hotel keeper had dragged her by it when she was refused entrance on her way home accompanying her husband's coffin was highly praised by the Confucian males, and was only one of many such incidents recorded in the well-known *Biographies of Virtuous Women*, a collection of stories of women who distinguished themselves by committing suicide after their husbands' deaths to guard their chastity and purity.

This doctrine of chaste widowhood became an official institution during the Ming Dynasty (1368–1643). Women who kept their widowhood despite their age were officially honored. Those who never consummated marriage because their fiances died were treated as widows, too, and remained "widows" the rest of their lives. Furthermore, chaste widowhood lent honor not only to the husband's family but also to his clan and the whole village. As a result, it became a common practice for women to be forced to commit suicide after their husbands' deaths. At the turn of the century, Confucianism was called "the man-eating religion." Perhaps a better term for it would be "woman-eating religion."

Perhaps because the Chinese social system was originally matriarchal, the mother in a family was respected. One of the Confucian doctrines, *xiao*, demands "loyalty and reverence toward one's parents." The mother, especially after her husband died, held considerable power and control in the family, even over its male members. One word from the mother could bring her sons to their knees. Even the Emperors, most of whom were advocates of Confucianism, had to kneel down to pay respect to their mothers, in fear of being accused of disrespect toward her.

However, the mother was powerful and honored only because she was the person to produce sons to carry the family name. Her power lies solely behind the doors; she has no legal and property rights. Put in other words, Confucianism acknowledges women only for the purpose of reproduction. Once a woman failed to produce a son for the family, she was regarded to have committed the worst moral crime, because, according to Confucius himself, among the three important reasons one can be accused of *bu xiao* (failure of the filial piety), the worst is being unable to produce a son for the family.

Toward the end of the nineteenth century, capitalism began to penetrate China, bringing with it conflicting socialist, anarchist, libertarian, and democratic ideologies into the troubled land. This influx of ideas eventually led to the bourgeois revolution of 1912 and the May 4th Movement of 1919, eroding the oppression of women. In the late 1800s, prominent liberal male reformers like Liang Qichao and Kang Youwei championed the idea of female equality and proposed important changes to enforce it. Roxane Witke (1973), an important woman scholar in Asian studies, notes:

> Beginning in the late Ch'ing [the turn of the century] the social role of women became one of the most prominent subjects of reform literature. Almost all major writers from then on addressed themselves to it, for it was the nexus of all questions of social change in China's recent history. (8)

Issues concerning women, such as the reform of the family system, the reform of marriage, divorce, chastity, suicide, suffrage, and the education of women, were dealt with, attacking the old values of Confucianism. One of the famous slogans of the May 4th Movement, an anti-imperialist, anti-feudal movement, was "Down with the Confucianism."

However, one cannot expect to wipe out the Confucian concept of women by one political campaign, which, as noted by Julia Kristeva, "is itself stained with unconscious vestiges of the old days" (95). These concepts and doctrines produced, in Chinese society, a series of social practices concerning women, within which Buck's female characters live.

Social Customs and Practices

Confucianism seems to have assigned three roles to a Chinese woman: the sexual object and possession of the man, the childbearing tool to carry on her husband's family name, and the servant to the whole family. This can be seen, first of all, in the way she was addressed. After her marriage, a woman became nameless. She was addressed by the role she played in the family. If she was married to the Wang family, she would be called Wang Jia Xifu (the daughter-in-law of the Wang family) when young, Wang Saozi (the big sister-in-law of the Wang family) once she reached her thirties, and Wang Da Ma (the big mother of the Wang family) beginning from her forties. Her given name and her maiden name were completely forgotten. She would be referred to by her husband to others as *Nei Ren*, an euphemism for wife, which literally means "inside person" or "person inside home."

Second, there are sayings, phrases, and proverbs that reveal how women have been viewed by society. While a woman is regarded as a sexual object for her man's enjoyment, it is always the woman's fault if the man overindulges himself in her, thus leading to the failure of his duty or career. Hence there is a phrase *Hong yan huo shui,* meaning "Beauty is the troubled water that brings disasters." Another proverb states that "Beauty is the skeleton with flesh."

The treatment of women by society is also reflected in the Chinese language itself. The word *lihun* (divorce) did not come into the Chinese lexicon until the 1920s. Before that, one could only find *xiu,* the closest equivelant to "divoice," which literally means "a man getting rid of his wife," or "sending the wife back to her own home."

At the morphological level, we find that the Chinese word for male is 男, which is made up of two parts. The upper part, 田, means "field" and the lower one, 力, means "strength." The word, therefore, means "one who works in the field," which was later semantically expanded to mean one who works outside. The word for female, 女, pictorially symbolizes a person who sits on her crossed legs, and the word for woman is 婦, the combination of "female" and "broom", suggesting that a woman was supposed to be always confined to the home, doing housework. The word for entertainment is 娱, the left part meaning "female." Similarly, the word for wonderful is 妙, which, taken apart, 少 女, means "young women." Clearly, Chinese women were sexual objects for men.

However, a woman's roles in Chinese society are best seen in how she lived her life. The following is a brief sketch of a woman's life in old China, divided into three stages: as a girl, as a wife, and as a mother.

The birth of a girl in a traditional Chinese family was never as welcomed as that of a boy. The birth of a boy was called "big happiness" while the birth of a girl is called "small happiness." If the firstborn was a girl, it would be a great disappointment to the family. If the second child were also a girl, the family would grieve, and the birth of a third daughter in line would be a tragedy for the family and disastrous to the mother, who would be blamed and despised. This was because a daughter was normally married off in her teens, when she was becoming most useful. As the old Chinese saying goes: "A married daughter is like the water that is thrown out of doors." She legally no longer belonged to her parent's family. Therefore, her upbringing expense could not be recouped. As Margery Wolf (1985) puts it:

Daughters were goods on which one lost money. They could contribute little or nothing to their natal families in the way of enhancing their status, increasing their wealth, or providing for their care in their old age. (1–2)

Women were victims of discrimination from the very moment of their births. Because of this, an infant girl, especially in a poor family faced with desperate financial difficulties, could be smothered to death at birth or sold at a very early age.

If they were fortunate enough to live, girls would experience a different process of upbringing from boys. From the very beginning of her life, a girl was made very aware of women's place at home by the notorious practice of footbinding, a symbol of seclusion and suppression. This binding process, which began in early childhood between ages one and three, inflicted unimaginable pain and ended in permanent crippling. The outcome of it was a bound foot reduced to three inches in length from heel to toe, with the toes bent under the sole. The procedure, usually performed by the mother, lasted ten to fifteen years, and after that, the feet had to remain bound for the rest of the woman's life. The only reward of it is the appreciation of men, which would supposedly result in the woman's pride and self-assurance.

The custom is believed to have started in the beginning of the tenth century, between the end of the Tang Dynasty (906) and the beginning of the Song Dynasty (960). It began as a fashion with the aristocracy in the royal court and then was imitated by the public and set as a custom, spreading throughout the nation. Such a foot was euphemistically called "golden lily," or "fragrant lily," and was thus enabled to enter courtly literature and to be sung about as a love fetish, setting off waves of adoration among poets. Here, as Lin (1935) reminds us, the word "fragrant" is significant, for it suggests the voluptuous atmosphere of the rich, whose chambers were filled with rare and fine perfume, as described often in Buck's novels about families of wealth.

Such a product of cruelty, of women's tears and suffering, had come to be greatly admired, played with, and worshiped by men. It became the most erotic organ of the female body. Having such a pair of small, crippled feet, with its little staggering dance-like steps, was an agreed beauty of a woman and sometimes the sole standard by which a man chose a wife. Men would simply not marry a woman with natural, unbound feet. A girl who refused such binding would be told that if she did not do it, no man would want her. All of that ordeal was to prepare a girl for her marriage. As Kristeva (1974) says:

> It is not at all shocking that women of many classes rush to submit themselves to the torture: after so many years of suffering, it presents a unique

opportunity to gain the respect and recognition of the in-laws, who will praise the beautiful tiny feet even beyond her dowry, as an undeniable proof of her capacity to suffer and obey. (82)

The coming of fashion of bound feet has often been compared with the fashion of narrow waists among European women, but the footbinding is obviously much more cruel. Fortunately, the footbinding was only popular in the cities with rich and well-to-do families. The poor, the servant girl, and the woman in the countryside could not afford such "beauty," for they had to labor to make ends meet. But their big feet would be looked down upon, being a sign of their humble origin and low social status.

Beside the footbinding, there were many strict rules for girls. Lin has given us an accurate and detailed account:

> The girl in any case had less of a childhood than the boy, and from the age of fourteen she began to seclude herself and learn the manners of womanliness, for the Chinese conception emphasizes the womanly woman: She rises earlier than her brothers, dresses more neatly than they, helps in the kitchen and often helps to feed her younger brothers. She plays with fewer toys, does more work, talks more quietly, walks about more delicately, and sits more properly, with her legs close together. She learns, above all, demureness, at the cost of sprightliness. Something of the childish fun and tomfoolery goes out of her, and she does not laugh but only smiles. She is conscious of her virginity, and virginity in old China was a possession more precious than all the learning of the world. She does not easily let strangers see her, although she often peeps from behind the partitions. She cultivates the charm of mystery and distance, and the more she is secluded the more she is worth. Actually, in a man's mind a lady shut up in a medieval castle is more enchanting than a girl you daily see face to face across the lunch counter. She learns embroidery, and with her young eyes and adroit fingers, she does excellent work and gets along much faster than she would in trigonometry. The embroidery is pleasant because it gives her time to dream, and youth always dreams. Thus she is prepared for the responsibilities of wifehood and motherhood. (153)

Since Confucius said that "[t]he virtue of a woman is her lack of knowledge and talent," women were not supposed to receive education of any kind. Until the 1920s, practically no women had gone to school. A well-known love story, "Liang Sanbo and Zhu Yingtai," tells how the heroine, Zhu Yingtai, has to disguise herself as a boy in order to go to a private school, where she falls in love with the hero Liang Sanbo, her classmate.

Though girls from educated families, like Madame Wu in Buck's *Pavilion of Woman*, did learn to read and write, the content of their education was primarily the Confucian classics, from which they may gain a glimpse of literature, history, and human wisdom.

There is no denying the fact that there have always been talented women in China. Even servants, such as Peony in Buck's *Peony*, learned to read and write from their masters. But the learning of these talented women was not of any use in the outside world. A good breeding ensured a better chance of success as wife and mother only. And some women's learning—poetry and painting mainly—was used to entertain men behind the door of the bedchamber or, worse, in a courtesan house.

Once a girl got married, her life became more difficult. To begin with, marriages were arranged by parents through matchmakers, which is still the case in some rural areas. It was not uncommon to marry a child before he or she was born. Marriage was a matter of "parents' order and matchmaker's words," an everyday idiom in the Chinese language. This was actually not as absurd as a Western reader might find: Because of the Confucian practice of seclusion of the male and female until they reached adulthood, young men and women had very limited opportunities to get acquainted with members of the other sex. Therefore, the parents would be the best decision makers on their marriages.

Even after engagement, a woman was not supposed to set eyes on her future husband until her wedding day. Whoever the man she happened to marry, he was her man for the rest of her life.

Once married, the bride was supposed to know how to behave toward her husband's family. She not only had to please her husband, but also his siblings and parents. She needed to pay special attention to pleasing her mother-in-law, who occupied a powerful position in the family. She had to be sweet and avoid being talkative so as not to cause or be involved in any trouble. If she was lucky enough to gain her husband's favor, she had to be very careful not to show too much happiness or boast about it, lest the mother-in-law should feel her own favor from the son endangered. When wronged, she could by no means talk back to the mother-in-law nor show any feeling of anger. She had to be very cautious with the sisters-in-law as well, who may be jealous of any act that might indicate favoritism on the mother's side. If she was the youngest wife, she had to listen to the older wives, too.

In day-to-day life, the wife was the first one to get up in the morning to prepare breakfast and to wait on the husband and parents-in-law if the family did not have a maid; she was the last one to go to bed at night after seeing to it that every thing was settled. This can be seen in detail in Buck's *The Good Earth.*

Thus, once married, a woman, in a way, became homeless. She was "a polite stranger to her husband, threatening in no way the emotional bond between mother and son or the cool respect between father and son" (Wolf 1985, 7). If the husband did not like her, she could be physically abused. She had nowhere to turn for help, as there was no protection of any kind, legal or otherwise. She, the abused, was often to be blamed for the mistreatment and, if the family was rich, the man could get another wife.

Most importantly, however, the wife was supposed to bear a son for the family, preferably within a year. If not, no matter how well she did in everything else, she would lose favor and face hostility and humiliation. If, after years, she still showed no hope of ever bearing a male child, she was to be blamed for failing to carry on the family name. She could be sent back to her parents' home, if they would take her back, as a way of humiliation, or simply be discarded or sold. The man would then have the duty to take another wife or a concubine. Sometimes the wife herself would assume the task of finding one for her husband, as Madame Wu does in *Pavilion of Woman*, and which was considered to be a virtue on the part of the wife. A man in a rich family could have several concubines, called "small wives," to be distinguished from the "original wife," "big wife," or "the first lady."

In the extended family of the rich class, it was common practice until the first quarter of this century for multiple wives to live together in the house. Buck describes such families and their problems in many of her works, including *East Wind: West Wind, Pavilion of Woman,* and *The Good Earth.*

It was customary for a couple to share residence and to have a common budget with their unmarried children and their male descendants' immediate families. Such families were considered a Confucian ideal. If a family could be *si shi tong tang* (having four generations under one roof), as the Chinese saying goes, the family head would be very happy because he or she had lived long enough to see it. However, such families provided a great many problems for all, particularly the wives.

Since there was no such thing as divorce, concubinage, as Lin (1935) said, "in a way takes the place of divorce in Western countries" to solve the complicated familial and social problem. Therefore, "marriage is the safest protection for women, and whenever men's morals relax it is the women who suffer, whether it be through divorce, concubinage, companionate marriage or free love" (163).

In fact, the husband did not have to have a reason for taking concubines. He could, through no "fault" whatsoever on the wife's part, but simply for his own sexual pleasure, have found a woman outside, very often in a house of prostitution, and take her home for a concubine. The new wife had to show respect for the first wife in public. Usually, the one that first bore a male child for the family would be the proudest. Once a wife lost her husband's favor, her life would be spent in loneliness, misery, and constant jealousy, and thus in fighting with other wives for the favor of both the husband and the parents-in-law. As a way out of her emotional desperation, she may choose to commit suicide, as depicted in Buck's *East Wind: West Wind* and in other Chinese novels such as *Family* and *The Dream of the Red Mansion*.

Once a wife became a mother, her position changed drastically. She would enjoy a status much higher than that of a wife, and perhaps higher than a mother in Western societies. This is because the Confucian moral codes dictate that one should respect, obey, and do his or her duty to the parents. A man's two great virtues, according to Confucianism, were *zhong* and *xiao* (loyalty and filial piety). As a result,

> A woman who survived to the third stage of life [motherhood] was, theoretically at least, in a fairly secure position, for the balance of one set of obligations, that between the young and the old, had tipped in her favor. The Three Obediences might require her to obey her adult son, but rarely would a son risk the social opprobrium that would result from neglecting or mistreating his aged mother. (Wolf 1985, 4)

Though, as an old Chinese saying goes, "If the son misbehaves or shows no manners, it is the father's fault," the burden of the actual day-to-day education of the children fell on the mother's shoulders, as the man was busy taking care of things in the outside world. She watched over their moral behavior, made sure the boys did their lessons, and some talented women actually took upon themselves the task of teaching their sons to read and write from an early age.

The mother could then speak up for the children's interests, and when the children grew up, she could speak through them. What is more, the mother often held the responsibility of finding wives for her sons and husbands for her daughters. One of the reasons that the mother was given such an important role was that the marriage was usually arranged through the matchmaker. Since matchmakers were usually women, it was considered improper for them to talk, at least not alone, with the fathers.

The lucky mother who had sons would now finally become a mother-in-law after arranging their marriage. A mother-in-law held even greater power than a mother. In extended families with all the sons, wives, and the grand-children living together, the mother-in-law, though still subordinate to the husband, had the power of ordering the daughters-in-law around. When the daughters-in-law had problems with each other, the mother-in-law's word would be final in settling matters. If she did not like a daughter-in-law, she could force the son to send her back to her own family.

If the mother-in-law outlived her husband, she would become the supreme power in the family, having considerable control over all domestic affairs, including the male members, though outwardly her eldest son was the head. Through the son her wishes were expressed. Such feminine power is best seen in the novel *The Dream of the Red Chamber*, perhaps the best known Chinese classic to deal with domestic issues, inter/intra-family relationships, and problems of an extended noble family. As noted by Kristeva (1974):

> It emphasizes at once the fragility and submissiveness of the young women, and the omnipotence of the old mother. One is struck by the authoritarian—even virile—aspect of this power of the first-wife-become-grandmother-of-the-family. (79)

Lastly, I should note that, with the coming of the Western ideas and the downfall of Confucianism in the end of the nineteenth century, considerable changes in ideology and social practice began to take place. The idea of sexual equality was being demanded and the chaste widowhood and double sex standard were denounced. The custom of arranged marriage was criticized and free love encouraged. The concubinage system was done away with. Bound feet were all of a sudden out of fashion. With the rising textile industry, many women could go out and work. Divorce became possible, though not encouraged. The seclusion of women was no longer practiced.

There came also schools for women. The first group of girls were admitted to the Peking National University in 1919, followed by coeducation in almost all colleges. Educated women began to participate in politics and many became revolutionists and even soldiers fighting side by side with men during the Sino-Japanese War.

Along with all the changes, there emerged many problems concerning women as the old customs clashed with the new. The old-fashioned women with bound feet were looked down upon. Many young people rebelled against the parents for the arranged marriage and wanted to choose their own partners. Some young lovers would run away from homes to escape the arranged marriage. Though concubinage was abandoned, "these old fashioned wives," as Buck (1931) pointed out so keenly, would take on extramarital relationships or renounce their feelings and live as before. "In either case the woman suffers, for the first relationship gives her no stability of position and the second is difficult in its loneliness" (907).

One could imagine the difficulty facing both the modern woman and the old-fashioned wife. The former, who was not legally married to the man she loved, would have to live a secret life or suffer from a bad reputation, for extramarital affairs were always, and still are, condemned, and the blame was rested almost always on women. The latter, whose whole training has been for the narrow, close life of a certain type of home, found it too late to go into any other sort of training. Therefore, Buck remarks: "When she is sent forth, she is sent forth literally into wilderness" (908).

The old large extended family also began to collapse. As Kristeva points out, "This crisis of the Chinese family and of patriarchal morality shattered the contractual peace of the *jia* with a passion whose tragic force has suggested comparison with early Greek drama" (97).

The crisis of the family and the dilemma for both men and women are very much reflected in the new Chinese literature, such as *The Storm*, a haunting play by Cao Yu. This tragic play portrays two love affairs, one between a son and his father's young small wife and the other between the second son (of the small wife) and the house maid, who turned out to be an illegitimate daughter of the father. All ends in a storm of death—the elder son commits suicide; the maid is killed by a dangling electric wire; and the second son dies through a desperate effort to rescue the maid, his lover and half sister.

Woman's condition in China has drastically changed since 1949, when the Communist government took over China's mainland. The government has made efforts to ensure that women get equal access to education, employment, and participation in all social activities. A woman now enjoys maternity leave with pay, and a salary equal to that of her male colleagues. She can choose her husband, divorce, and remarry. However, one should not view China as a woman's paradise: traditional ideas, which have dominated for over two thousand years, cannot be expected to be eradicated overnight.

In the following three chapters, I will show how Buck has portrayed Chinese women, both in urban and rural areas, both aristocratic women and women of humble origins, in their struggle to achieve freedom, dignity, and happiness within the social context discussed in this chapter. These women are different individuals, but they have profound and significant similarities. They may take different routes in their respective lives and arrive at different destinations, but the driving force in their lives is the same. By offering us a wide array of characters different in appearance, personality traits, and under different social and familial conditions, Buck trusts us to discover the good qualities that exist in all of them. This does not only illustrate Buck's understanding of and love for her Chinese women characters, but also contributes to her success of characterization.

3

Aristocratic Women

THIS CHAPTER ANALYZES THE CHARACTERIZATION IN *EAST WIND: WEST WIND* AND *Pavilion of Women*. These two novels are similar in two ways. First, they are both about Chinese aristocratic women in cities as opposed to peasant women in the countryside as in *The Good Earth* and *The Mother*. As women of wealthy, socially prominent families, the characters in the novels do not have to worry about their basic survival. Second, the characters face a need to adapt to the changing time: Kwei-lan, in *East Wind: West Wind*, has to adjust herself to her American-educated husband with Western ideas; Madame Wu, in *Pavilion of Women*, has to cope with her youngest son, Fengmo, who has adopted many new ideas and later decides to run schools to educate children rather than manage the family business as expected of a traditional aristocratic man.

It will be argued that Madame Wu is more individualized than Kwei-lan. In fact, Madame Wu is the most individualized character among all analyzed in this study. Besides, both Kwei-lan and Madame Wu are able to use their power, sometimes in manners that seem manipulative, to achieve what they deserve, although their ways of doing so are much different.

East Wind: West Wind

East Wind: West Wind is Pearl S. Buck's first novel. Though short and simple, it is viewed as "a tale of absolute distinction" (A. C. 1930, 8), exquisitely written with delicacy and charm. It is set in China's aristocratic society at a time when the West wind had for the first time begun to sweep over the ancient China, shaking the innermost life behind the closed doors of the feudal families. The East, with its thousand years of traditions, had met a real challenge of Western civilization.

It is against this background that the Chinese women in *East Wind: West Wind* are portrayed.

The novel is narrated in the first person. Kwei-lan, the protagonist, tells of the arising conflicts brought to her and her family by the wind of Western civilization. Daughter of a rich government official, Kwei-lan was betrothed to her husband before she was born and has been reared during all her girlhood for the single purpose of marriage. However, her husband, who has been in America for twelve years as a medical student, does not seem to find her attractive in her silent obedience, and sees no beauty in her bound feet. To gain his love, therefore, she finds that the only way out is to yield to her husband's new ways, and to do as he wishes. Fortunately, once she shows willingness to change, her husband is there to help. Just as she has gone through much pain and finally gained favor from her husband, thus settling her own problem, her brother, having been to America to study science, brings back an American girl to be his wife. This creates much conflict and pain in her parents' family. Kwei-lan, in helping to deal with the problem and getting to know the American sister-in-law, gains more knowledge and understanding of people at large and sets her eyes to the future, while her mother sternly sticks to her age-old beliefs and refuses until her death to accept a foreign daughter-in-law, even at the risk of renouncing the heritage of her only son.

A *New York Times* review says the following about the novel:

> [It] involves consideration of two problems, immediate and sternly practical. These problems are miscegenation between the white and yellow race and the internal rift caused by the revolt of Western educated young men against tradition, against the social and family systems sanctified by the customs of a thousand years. ("Chinese Life" 1930, 8)

Upon its publication, *East Wind: West Wind* won mostly praises. *Pacific Affairs* carried a short review saying that "The book is sheer drama—quiet, strong, infinitely moving" and believed the novel has given "the surest key that has been given the West for the understanding of the East" (E. G. 1930, 506). Nathaniel Peffer (1930) admires Buck's knowledge of China, although he is mistaken about her birthplace: "Mrs. Buck knows her China intuitively, and it is not necessary to read her biographical notice on the jacket to know that she was born there." He goes on to say that Buck "tells more of contemporary China than a year of newspaper headlines or a shelf of volumes by politically minded experts, and tells it entertainingly" (6). Edwin Seaver (1930) praises it as "a novel off the beaten path" (10m). The *New York Times* review rightly stated that:

> Only one who, like the author, has lived all her life in China, yet being American still holds to Western concepts of romantic love, marriage and the scope of filial duty—only a lover of China, but no convert to her code of family and clan supremacy over the individual, could have written this beautiful novel. ("Chinese Life" 1930, 8)

However, the *New Republic* carried a very short review by Isidore Schneider (1930), who thinks the novel "empty of any lifelikeness in its characters or significance in its thesis—the clash between modern and traditional China" (24). This criticism will be refuted in the following discussion, which will show that Buck's characters in this novel are anything but empty of lifelikeness.

No critic seems to have given much thought to the novel's subtitle: "A Chinese Woman Speaks." But it is of significance. It reveals Buck's intention to let the reader know China through the eyes of a woman and the Chinese people through the images of their female representatives, whom Buck always believed to possess the finest quality that can be possessed. Moreover, women's problems were a key issue in China at the turn of the century. With the Western influence, the women's liberation movement had just begun to rise. Educated women welcomed the change with open arms, demanding more freedom and equality with men. The uneducated women, who had seldom been outside their courtyard gates, however, found the idea of equality of little significance and too far from their daily life. Caught in the whirlwind of the East and West, Chinese women were the ones who had the most difficulty in coping, for they had been bound most tightly by the thousand years of tradition and would not know how to change and how to survive in the outside world even if they wanted to. For many women, tragedy and triumph went side by side. If one failed to survive the whirlwind, she would be discarded by it, thus becoming a victim of the change.

Living in China in the middle of the whirlwind, Buck understood the significance and the inevitability of the change. Out of sympathy for Chinese women, she felt strongly that she should tell the world about this time of change (Buck 1954, 164–66). This she did in successfully depicting women in one family, especially Kwei-lan and her mother, and their struggle in the whirlwind, providing the reader with a microscope to view women's conditions in China at the turn of the century.

The analysis of characterization in this section concentrates on Kwei-lan and, to a lesser degree, Kwei-lan's mother, the former an embodiment of adaptation and the latter an embodiment of resistance. As a character, Kwei-lan is very typical of the women in her time, although she is individual enough to be a successful, memorable character. Kwei-lan's process of changing is a painful one, but typical and representative of the process the whole nation was undergoing. It was forced, agonizing, but for the better. In this process, Kwei-lan has to give up her power, which she has gained from her extensive traditional training. However, this is not, as it may appear at first sight, at odds with the characteristic of other women characters who use their power to achieve what they deserve, because in Kwei-lan's case the surrender of the old power means the gaining of a new power while holding onto it means the complete loss of it, without anything to be gained in return.

Kwei-lan's mother, on the other hand, represents those who refused to change, clinging to the old, which was no longer suitable for the changing China. By so doing, they fell victims to change, thus failing to survive the inevitable conflict, getting swallowed in the whirlwind of the two worlds.

It is also my contention that characterization plays a vital role in bringing out the theme of the novel. It is through the characterization, particularly of Kwei-lan and her mother, that the clash between Eastern and Western civilizations, between the traditional China and the modern China, and between the old and young generations is depicted.

At the beginning of the novel, the reader learns that Kwei-lan has been newly married. Just as for any woman, her marriage is an important turning point in her life. Unlike most women's marriage, however, hers comes with ramifications and consequences that go beyond a personal and familiar nature.

Buck makes a painstaking effort to describe Kwei-lan's pre-marriage life. First, we see Kwei-lan's family background. Kwei-lan's father has four wives, her mother being the First Lady who runs the family while her father is often on his many tours outside. Except for her mother—who, having long lost hope with her husband, places all her hope on the children—all the other three concubines' lives have been focused on competing for the husband's favor, which they have lost when their brief beauty was gone. However, they never want to admit this painful fact, even to themselves, for once they lose their husband's favor, they are little more than slaves in the family. Even the servants are contemptuous of them.

This background, realistic and truthful to women's conditions in China at the time, is significant in setting the stage for Kwei-lan's traditional training.

Knowing that, without winning and maintaining the husband's favor, a woman would have no happiness and dignity to speak of, Kwei-lan's mother spares no effort in training Kwei-lan, enabling her to please her future husband when she is wed.

Thus the training begins. At the age of six, Kwei-lan is separated from her brother, who was then nine, for it is considered improper for them to play together anymore. He is removed to the court of men, which Kwei-lan is forbidden to enter. From then on, her sole task is preparing, in both mind and body, for the marriage, for serving her future husband and mother-in-law. For her husband, her mother teaches her how to decorate herself to draw his attention, how to cook to tempt his appetite, and how to speak with her eyes and facial expressions rather than words. She is even taught to play the ancient harp and to sing verses by famous ancient poets for his delight. To help in her future relationship with her mother-in-law, she is taught how to prepare and present tea to an elder, how to stand in an elder's presence, how to listen in silence either at praise or blame. She is to submit herself "as a flower submits to sun and rain alike" (9). Above all, her mother binds her feet to be smaller than those of any woman in her generation. In one word, Kwei-lan has been reared "in all the honored traditions" (4) and "well versed in all the duties of a gentle woman" (10). Her mother is confident that not even her future mother-in-law could possibly find anything lacking. Counting all the odds, Kwei-lan is bound to succeed in her marriage, unless she should bear no son. The path of her life seems to be well established and Kwei-lan accepts it, having no other alternatives: "I am the daughter of an old Chinese house, with old customs, old furniture, old well-tried relationships, safe, sure! I know how to live there!" (65).

Here, Kwei-lan's family clearly represents the two thousand years of the feudalist belief that a woman exists only for the pleasure of men. This belief molded women into a particular type, making them ideal wives in the Confucian codes. Kwei-lan is portrayed, up until this point in the novel, as such a typical woman, perfectly in line with Confucian standards. If the molding of women into a source of pleasure for their husbands was unfair and tragic, the impact this tradition had on women's way of thinking was even more disturbing. They generally did not realize that they were victims of such prejudice and mistreatment. On the contrary, they were led to believe that because this had been the way for thousands of years, it should be the way forever. Kwei-lan, for instance, is contented and happy, because this is how her people have "lived in quietness and dignity, confident of their rectitude" (3). She knows no other way of living her life:

I never dreamed I could wish to be different. Without thinking on the matter it seemed to me that as I was, so were all those who were really people. If I had heard faintly, as from the distance outside the courtyard walls, of women not like myself, women who came and went freely like men, I did not consider them. I went, as I was taught, in the approved ways of my ancestors. Nothing from the outside ever touched me. I desired nothing. (4)

There seem to be some good reasons for Buck to depict the premarital Kwei-lan as a typical traditional woman. Against this typicality, Buck will, in the bulk of the book, weave and carve her main character, gradually individualizing her. It also helps Buck to expand the theme of change beyond that of an individual to that of the type—Chinese women at the time, and even to the Chinese people in general.

The typical training Kwei-lan has had is, however, soon to be challenged. Her peaceful mind is first stirred by the West wind that comes with the return of her betrothed from abroad just before her marriage. She learns with astonishment that her betrothed wishes to break their engagement because she is uneducated and has bound feet. She denies the truthfulness of the news with her deep-rooted belief that there could be nothing wrong in her being formally "uneducated," for the possession of knowledge has never accompanied beauty in women and only farmers and servants have big, natural feet. Moreover, the seventeen years of wifehood preparation *is* education, though in a different sense.

However painful it is, Kwei-Lan could no longer deny the truth once she meets her husband for the first time on the wedding night. In his "stiff, black, foreign clothes" (34), he shows clearly that he has not wished to marry her. Seeing her reluctance in giving her own hand to him, which she does according to her mother's advice of being chill rather than warm, he assumes that they are both forced into the marriage. But she sees no force at all, for

what else could I do if I did not marry? And how could I marry except as my parents arranged it? Whom could I marry if not the man to whom I had been betrothed all my life? It was all according to our custom. (37)

Kwei-Lan becomes more confused when her husband declares that he wishes to follow the new ways: to regard her in all things as his equal and to encourage her to embark the new path with him. She is amazed beyond understanding. To her mind, a wife can never be equal with her husband. Once married, her husband naturally becomes her master. As for the new path, she has no idea what lies ahead. On her wedding night, her husband leaves her alone in the bridal chamber, the marriage unconsummated.

For the first time in her life, Kwei-lan's hard-learned traditional ways are being challenged and her value system is turned upside down by the very person she is so prepared to serve. Feeling unwanted, Kwei-lan is bewildered, desperate, terrified, and hurt. What is worse, "there could never be any return" (38) for her. She knows that if, even by miracle, she were to find her way home, her mother would be there waiting to send her back to her duty. She no longer belongs to her family. As the old saying goes, "A daughter married is the water poured out."

Henceforth begins Kwei-lan's new life. Their "honeymoon" turns out to be full of bitterness for her and trying for both of them. Her husband wages a war with the old and traditional. He has himself and Kwei-lan moved out of the courts of his parents' family, against the latter's wishes. He will not have her serve as a servant, even to his mother, who, he thinks, has enough servants anyway. Neither has he any interest in having her produce sons for the family as his parents command him to do. Unlike a gentleman in his position, he will not spend his days in dignified leisure at home, but wishes instead to work outside, using the knowledge he has learned from the West to serve his country. Furthermore, he has created a new environment, a home with foreign-looking furniture arranged in Western style. He is at work all day, leaving her alone in this strange home until evening. When he is home at night, he busies himself with books, never turning an eye on her.

From this we see the importance of Kwei-lan as a typical character. Her predicament is not individual, but typical of all those who were caught in the clash between the East and the West. It is not her personal family tradition that is being challenged, not her own value system that is being turned upside down, but the tradition of Chinese society and the values that have gradually been formed during its long history. In fact, Buck hints at this in the very first page of the novel where Kwei-lan tells her implied reader: "You know that for five hundred years my revered ancestors have lived in this age-old city of the Middle Kingdom. Not one of the august ones was modern; nor did he have a desire to change himself." Here the city is "age-old," China is referred to as the "Middle Kingdom," a nation that views itself as the center of the world, and the people living in it are so used to their old ways that they desire no change of any kind.

Therefore, when Kwei-lan's tradition is challenged, the whole Chinese society is challenged. The kind of problem Kwei-lan faces is also typical of the problems the Chinese people faced at the time: Because of the sweeping West wind, the Chinese found their long-formed traditions ignored, thought wrong, backward, and uncivilized, and thus abandoned. The Western thoughts and ideas forced themselves onto the East. This theme of importance is largely achieved through characterization, particularly through portraying Kwei-lan as a typical Chinese woman in a typical aristocratic family.

However, as the old traditions did not give up without fighting, Kwei-lan will not stop her efforts to gain her husband's favor. Having observed the ups and downs in the lives of all the women in her family, Kwei-lan is determined to use her cunning to search for a way to turn his eyes on her, but her efforts come to no avail. First, she tries to draw his attention to her beauty by carefully making up, but he makes it clear that he prefers women to appear natural. Then, she tries to cook food good enough for an emperor, only to find that after "his many years of feeding upon the barbarous and half-cooked fare of the Western peoples, he has lost his taste and cares no more for delicate food" (52). Her ability to play the harp does draw some attention from him, but he says that he will buy her a piano so that she can learn to play Western music as well.

Her failure is not at all surprising, for she is using what she has learned from the old tradition, which is exactly the root of the problem. On the surface, she is trying to survive the change, but, in essence, she is resisting it. However, these episodes reveal to us one of Kwei-lan's character traits: She is a woman of strength and determination. This is the first hint of individuality of Kwei-lan. Placed in such a whirlwind, Kwei-lan has two alternatives: to refuse to change or to adapt to change. It is clear to her that the former would keep her outside her husband's favor and her life would be miserable forever. Therefore, she decides on the latter alternative.

However, to change is no easy matter. It needs motivation, determination, endurance, help and encouragement, and rewarding results. Fortunately, Kwei-lan has all of these, and it is through a combination of all these factors that we see her individuality.

Kwei-lan's motivation comes from her desire to please her husband so as to achieve happiness, which, ironically, exemplifies a conviction that she has formed from her extensive wifehood training. She realizes that time has changed, her husband has changed, and if she does not want to be left out in the cold, she has to change herself. She is compelled to renounce her past and surrender. Her resolution to change does not come from within, but from external forces. Doan (1965) realizes this when he writes: "Kwei-lan may well represent the soul of ancient China: though she becomes a convert to modern life, the conversion is forced upon her by marriage rather than by a genuine conviction" (47).

Thus begins Kwei-lan's readjustment, an initiation into her husband's world, a world of the new. The most symbolic part of this process is the unbinding of her feet. The binding of her feet was done for the sole reason of pleasing her husband, who now finds the small bound feet most disturbing because his Western medical training tells him that those "three-inch golden lilies" are unhealthy to her body. Therefore he wants them to be unbound. Kwei-lan refuses to do so but, after all her other efforts fail to turn him to her, reluctantly agrees.

The loosening of the feet is accompanied by an intolerable pain:

> There were times in the day when I tore at the bandages to unfasten them and bind them more tightly to ease me; and then the thought of my husband and that he would know at night made me replace them with trembling hands. The only slight respite I could get was to sit on my feet and rock back and forth. (84)

The symbolic nature of this process is seen in several ways. First, it illustrates the difference between Kwei-lan and her husband. To him, the unbinding is a resolution to break away from the old, a challenge to the Confucian moral codes: "It is not only for us but for others, too—a protest against an old and wicked thing." This reflects the result of his Western education, his conscious rebellion against the East wind. However, the social implication of this is not appreciated by Kwei-lan: "No! I do it only for you—to be a modern woman for you!" (85). To Kwei-lan, then, what motivates the change is her long-held conviction that the happiness of a woman lies only in her ability to please her husband, a prerequisite to gaining and maintaining his favor.

The unbinding of feet is symbolic also in that it is as painful as the binding itself. While the binding process symbolizes the oppression and confinement of Chinese women, molding them into a type in accordance with Confucian standards, the unbinding symbolizes the breaking away from that tradition, moving toward a new way of life. It suggests that such a change is no easy endeavor: It is as difficult to get out of the mold as getting into it. New things are seldom if ever within easy reach. Kwei-lan has sacrificed to fit into the mold, but now that sacrifice is rendered "useless" and "new sacrifice" (84) has to be made. The pain involved in such a process is not physical only. It is also mental, psychological, and spiritual. By adopting new ways of life, Kwei-lan is abandoning her seventeen years of feudal education, which has fostered in her mind ways of thinking, ways of viewing the world, as well as ways of behavior. While the physical pain is felt by the senses, the psychological and spiritual pain is felt, though subconsciously, by the mind. The pain in the mind is undoubtedly more painful than the pain in the body.

Another important factor in Kwei-lan's success is that her efforts to change are rewarded. Once the process begins, "a complete new life poured in" and she feels a sense of freedom, both physical and psychological. Physically, she begins to find it easier to move around and is eventually able to run, something she would not have been able to do with her "golden lilies." Psychologically, she and her husband begin to have a common goal: to go through the pain of the unbinding together. He starts to share his Western experience with her, which she learns as eagerly as a child. With the gradual building up of mutual understanding between them, love comes into their young hearts. Kwei-lan ceases to be lonely and feels happy now, even feeling good to be a little modern. Wherever her husband is becomes her home and their marriage is finally consummated.

The rewards of change serve as a source of encouragement for Kwei-lan, convincing her that she has made the right choice, although the motivation was initially to please her husband. By this, Buck perhaps means to indicate to us her view of resolving the clash between the two winds: One should not resist the change completely, neither should one abandon the tradition completely. The two cultures can help each other, complement each other, finally meeting somewhere in between and getting united. This becomes more obvious when Kwei-lan gives birth to a boy: it is a result of love that has developed between the couple during the process of change, and it is also a symbol of Kwei-lan's fulfillment of her greatest traditional duty to her husband.

From this we may say that Kwei-lan represents the new generation of China. She does not belong to those who, like her husband and her brother, are restless, impatient, and eager to turn the ancient China into a modern one overnight. Instead, she represents those who were realistic, who sympathized with the old and had gradually although reluctantly come to understand the new. Mrs. Liu, a friend of Kwei-lan's husband, who is among the few women to have received Western education, says it well: "Learn the good that you can of the foreign people and reject the unsuitable" (109). It is in this group of young Chinese that Buck sees hope for China.

"Frail" though she thinks she is, Kwei-lan serves as a "bridge, spanning the infinity between past and present." She says: "I clasp my mother's hand; I cannot let it go, for without me she is alone. But my husband's hand holds mine; his hand holds mine fast. I can never let love go" (167).

Kwei-lan's success also depends on her husband's support and under-standing. Without her husband, who takes her along the new path by pro-viding her with opportunities to learn and experience new ways of life, she would have been discarded by time.

In the process of learning, Kwei-lan's vision is expanded and she be-comes more understanding toward people in general. For example, she is able to see the good qualities that dwell in her American sister-in-law, through whom she learns that Western women have the same feelings as herself. Despite the difference in outer appearance, the same motherly in-ner feelings bring them together as friends.

A common characteristic among Buck's women characters—that they make the best use of the little power they had to achieve what they de-serve—seems absent in Kwei-lan, for she gives up her power rather than use it. This absence, however, is more apparent than real. Kwei-lan chooses to surrender her power because she sees it as a better alternative to obtain happiness. By so doing, she will be able to gain her husband's favor, thus achieving real happiness. Holding on to the power would mean living a life that is loveless and sorrowful and seeing the opportunity and hope for a better life evaporate. Simply put, giving up the old power means the gain-ing of new power. As happens in the latter part of the novel, Kwei-lan does gain such a power and lives a happy life. Therefore, we can say that giving up the old power is Kwei-lan's unique way of using it, her "underground" way to achieve what life offers her.

In contrast to Kwei-lan, who survives the conflict between the old and the new, is her mother, a typical traditional woman, who falls victim to the changing time. Kwei-lan's mother is depicted as a typical traditional First Lady. In appearance, she resembles the paintings of ancient women. "She understood many things and moved with a habitual, quiet dignity which kept the concubines and their children all fearful in her presence" (14). She seldom speaks except for the purpose of maintaining the old order in the house; when she does speak, she speaks in a most proper manner. She is wise, too: under her hands, her husband's money is never carelessly spent. Though she has lost her husband's favor long ago, she is able to maintain some respect from him for her faultless management of the house. As a mother, she is strict and responsible, bringing her children, particularly Kwei-lan, up according to Confucian standards without any compromise. Though formal in manner, she is kind to her children, caring very much about their well-being. Thus she is depicted as an ideal wife and mother, a typical traditional woman in an aristocratic family.

However, under the surface of her intense gravity there is a depth of sadness seen in her eyes, which are like "sad jewels . . . , dying from over-much knowledge of sorrow" (13). This sadness stems from "the anguish of a hundred generations of women who loved their lords and lost their favor" (162), a consequence of the unfair treatment of women in that society. As a result, she no longer believes that there is such a thing as genuine love between man and woman. She tells Kwei-lan bluntly: "Do not use poetic expressions in regard to it [love]. It is only desire—the man's desire for the woman, the woman's desire for a son. When that desire is satisfied, there is nothing left" (166).

This is Buck's condemnation of the mistreatment of women. The tradition of treating women as sex objects for men deprived women of love and, more sadly, of their hope of love, leaving them in serious doubt about the human capacity of loving.

Faced with the force of the West wind that spares no one, Kwei-lan's mother chooses to resist change. She does not approve of her son's going abroad to study medicine, is opposed to his marrying a foreign woman, and is greatly disappointed when her foreign daughter-in-law gives birth to a child. She refuses, until death, to recognize her only son as the heir in the family.

Kwei-lan's mother, however, is a more complicated character than this. While she refuses to give in to her son's Western ideas and ways of life, she approves Kwei-lan's change. In fact, it is she who convinces Kwei-lan that in order for her to gain the favor of her husband, she has to yield to his ways. She tells Kwei-lan:

> there is only one path in this world for a woman—only one path to follow at all costs. She must please her husband. It is more than I can bear that all my care for you must be undone. But you no longer belong to my family. You are your husband's. There is no choice left you save to be what he desires. — Yet, stay! . . . bend yourself to his will. (71)

She tells her even to unbind her feet, for "The times have changed" (71).

How can we explain this contradiction, then? The answer seems to lie in her traditional way of viewing life. She allows and supports Kwei-lan's change because she believes that a woman's happiness can be obtained only through her husband's favor, whatever kind of person he is and whatever he demands. She resists Kwei-lan's brother's marrying an American woman because such a marriage would break the family's arrangement of his marrying the daughter of Li, thus violating the Confucian morality of filial obedience and the age-old tradition that marriage should be based on parents' consent. Moreover, such a marriage "means that there will be no sons and grandsons proper to carry on ancestral worship in the house" (Doan 1965, 32). Thus we see that both the mother's refusal to recognize the son's change and support for her daughter's change find their roots in her traditional ideas, beliefs, and morality.

There is still another question, though. Since both Kwei-lan and her mother are seen as typical traditional women, why does Kwei-lan change to survive the East-West conflict while the mother refuses to give in, thus falling victim to it? There seem to be several reasons.

First, the two characters are at different stages of their lives. For Kwei-lan, life is just beginning, and the happiness of her life ahead depends solely on her relationship with her husband. Therefore, she sees the rewarding side of change and later tastes its sweetness. For the mother, however, there are no such rewards in sight. Love has long gone out of her life, and her only hope remaining is to see grandchildren to carry on the family name, to which her son's marrying an American poses a direct threat. Besides, giving in to her son's new ways means the giving up of her old beliefs and values, the beliefs and values that has taken her the entire life to foster.

Second, although both characters are typical traditional women, the degree to which they have committed themselves to the traditional beliefs seems different. It is true that Kwei-lan has been taught all the traditional values and learned the traditional ways. Only seventeen years old when she was married, she has not become a diehard believer of the old system. Still in the formative period of life, she is more ready to learn, to experience, and to adopt new ways of life from those of her mother. Once the process of change begins, she listens to her husband with interest and absorbs new ideas with an open heart. Her mother, on the other hand, is at an age when her values and beliefs are so deeply rooted that drastic changes are hard, if not impossible, to understand, to appreciate, even to tolerate, let alone to adapt to. For example, through her experience with her husband, who has four wives in the house, she decides that love is nothing but sexual desire. When she asks her son to marry the daughter of Li and take the American woman as a concubine, the son refuses on the ground that he does not love the daughter of Li. Given her experience, how can she take this as a legitimate reason?

The specific situations the two characters find themselves in comprise the third reason for their difference. After marriage, Kwei-lan is immediately placed in an environment where she is powerless, having to do things differently from the way she was taught. Her mother, on the other hand, remains in her house where she is in absolute control over everything, where she can survive somewhat without having to change.

Thus we see a tragic figure in Kwei-lan's mother, a character who lives a life of sorrow and dies with the death of the old system. The tragedy is that she insists until death on keeping the very system that has crushed her own happiness. Such a system treated her as a sex object to her husband, thus forming in her mind a twisted view of life. However, like most women of and before her times, she does not realize that she has been mistreated and oppressed. As a result, she becomes an instrument to maintain and perpetuate this system. By providing such a figure, therefore, Buck makes her readers see the power of the old system so that they can be more appreciative of those who fight against it.

The typicality of Kwei-lan's mother is seen more clearly when compared to Madame Wu in *Pavilion of Women*. They are both first ladies in the house. They are both hardworking, intelligent, and run their houses well. However, Kwei-lan's mother refuses to adapt to the changing time, while Madame Wu changes to fit it. There seem to be two reasons for this. The first reason is external: whereas Madame Wu has Brother Andrew to teach and enlighten her, Kwei-lan's mother does not have anyone to help her see the inevitability and benefit of change. Thus, Madame Wu gradually sees peace in the house and happiness in those around her, brought about by her adaptation to the changing time, but Kwei-lan's mother only sees the damages that change has brought to her family and to the old system she has been trying hard to maintain.

However important external forces may be, they can prove useless if the individual characters do not have any internal motivation for change, and such an internal difference is the second and more decisive factor in making Madame Wu and Kwei-lan's mother different. Madame Wu is portrayed, throughout the novel, as an extremely intelligent, well-read woman. She is philosophical and strives for internal peace and spiritual freedom. In fact, peace and freedom are to her the highest attainment of life. Therefore, Brother Andrew's theological teaching, which carries with it Western thinking and ideas, fulfills her needs, paving the way for her to act in ways called for by the changing time. Kwei-lan's mother, on the other hand, is not such a woman. While intelligent and capable, she does not bother herself with things such as spirituality and freedom. She devotes all her energy to keeping the family within the Confucian morality and order, and lacks any sort of readiness to change.

As literary characters, therefore, Kwei-lan's mother is typical while Madame Wu is very individualized. The typicality of Kwei-lan's mother seems to have two functions. First, she serves as a character to contrast Kwei-lan with so as to show the significance of Kwei-lan's effort to change. Second, she is a representative of those traditional women who were discarded by time. This illustrates Buck's skill in characterization: she is able to craft different characters out of similar molds.

Through Kwei-lan and her mother, as well as the other minor characters such as the three concubines, who also still live in the old ways, Buck presents the Western reader with the real conditions of China in a time of change. She demonstrates that changes in China are inevitable and difficult. Through her characters, Buck shows the reader that Chinese women are able to change with time and have the strength to endure the pain that comes with the process of change.

As a character, Kwei-lan does not lack individuality to be unique and memorable. In her, however, we see no shrewdness, profound thinking, or yearning for internal peace as we do in Madame Wu. We do not see as much diligence as in O-lan (*The Good Earth*). Neither do we see the kind of motherhood and womanhood as we do in the mother (*The Mother*). Compared to those characters, therefore, Kwei-lan is more typical than individualized. In fact, she falls more near the typicality end of the typicality–individuality continuum.

Kwei-lan's typicality, however, in no way indicates a failure of characterization on the part of the writer. On the contrary, it serves the theme of the novel well: With it, Buck shows how the Chinese people strived to adapt to the change of time and to survive the conflict between the East wind and the West; with it, Buck reveals her conviction that the two cultures can embrace each other rather than one completely obliterating the other.

Pavilion of Women

Unlike *The Good Earth* and *The Mother* (to be analyzed in chapter 5), in which we see Chinese peasant women's strength in their struggle to survive, and *East Wind: West Wind*, in which the heroine adapts herself to the changing environment, *Pavilion of Women* tells of a Chinese aristocratic woman's long and ardent path to freedom and internal peace.

Madame Wu is a highly individualized character. She uses the power invested in her by society to achieve her purpose of gaining spiritual freedom, and her way of doing so is marked by shrewdness and manipulation. Through her struggle, Buck shows Western readers that a Chinese woman, at that particular time in history, found it very difficult, in fact almost impossible, to gain freedom, regardless of how capable, intelligent, and spiritually oriented she was. Society had exerted its power and prejudices on her, chaining her with all kinds of earthly responsibilities that would consume her body and soul, leaving almost nothing for herself. The more she struggled, the tighter the chain became.

This section will concentrate on Buck's depiction of the oppression of Chinese women and Madame Wu's fight against such oppression. It will be demonstrated that Madame Wu is a highly individualized character and that Buck the writer fully understood the plight of Chinese women and had great sympathy toward them.

Since the novel is about women, Buck first provides us with a realistic picture of how Chinese women were oppressed and mistreated by society. For example, Madame Wu's mother's youngest sister "remained a virgin, because the man she had been about to marry had died" (13). She had to become a nun as a result. Moreover, in a rich family like Wu's, the wives do not breast-feed their children lest their breasts become less firm, so they hire milkmaids whose own children often go hungry (17). In such rich families, "[m]en and women eat at separate tables" (109). It was also a common practice for unhappy concubines in great houses to "hang themselves, or swallow their rings or eat raw opium" (133). All these facts are in line with the social conditions under which women lived as discussed in chapter 2, which indicates Buck's understanding of Chinese culture and her effort to provide a believable backdrop against which her main character will act.

The reader might find that Madame Wu is free from such mistreatment. There are two reasons for this. First, Madame Wu has reached mother-in-lawhood, which means, as seen previously, she has the power to oversee the operation of the family. Second, she is intelligent and capable, while her husband is almost a good-for-nothing. Therefore, she becomes the decision-maker and manager of the household, thus gaining the respect of all and escaping some of the mistreatment other women face.

That Madame Wu does not seem as much oppressed as other women is, upon closer examination, only a first-sight impression. In fact, she is very much oppressed, although her oppression is seen on a different dimension: in the difficulty of her endeavor to gain freedom, which is the theme of the novel.

Analyzing the character of Madame Wu, we find that her individuality lies in her power, strong will, eloquence, shrewdness, intelligence, and the respect and trust she is given by the whole family. It is true that one can find any one of these characteristics in many women; the combination of them can only be Madame Wu.

The most striking characteristic of Madame Wu is perhaps her power. She has power over everything and everybody. She is not only in charge of all events and activities in the family—supervising all servants, deciding on and presiding over family feasts, and allocating budgets to her sons' families—but also oversees the family business, deciding on what and when to grow in the fields and what and when to sell or purchase land and products. Moreover, it is by her hands that everyone's fate is controlled. She selects wives for all her sons, has the final say in what they will do in their lives, and, after her fortieth birthday, she decides that Mr. Wu is to take a concubine, which, she knows, he will do regardless of whether he agrees or not. All these she later finds out are wrongdoings, but they show her power nonetheless.

In a typical rich Chinese family at the time, the social practice of concubinage is the root of jealousy among the First Lady and concubines and creates family turbulence. This is summarized well in Madame Kang's words when she hears Madame Wu's idea of letting Mr. Wu take a concubine:

> Why, when my father took a concubine, my mother cried and tried to hang herself, and we had to watch her night and day and when he took a second concubine, the first one swallowed her earrings, and so it went when he had the five he ended with. They all hated one another and contended for him. (98)

But Madame Wu is Madame Wu. She arranges it anyway and her husband cannot disagree once she has made the decision. Madame Wu's power does not stop here. While, in usual practices, it is the husband that decides whom to take, in the Wu family, Madame Wu first comes out with a detailed mental picture of a woman who will suit Mr. Wu and the family best, and then finds Chiuming through a matchmaker. A more detailed discussion of this will follow later in this section.

One might wonder why Madame Wu has so much power while other women, as analyzed in other chapters, do not. There appear to be two reasons. First, as both the First Lady and later the mother-in-law of a rich, extended family, Madame Wu is bestowed with great responsibility for the whole family's welfare, thus helping to insulate her from the kind of oppression other women face. Second, her skills, strength, shrewdness, and ability help her to gain and to maintain power, which a woman of lesser qualities would not have been able to do.

First of all, Madame Wu is beautiful. Her beauty keeps Mr. Wu out of the flower house, a kind of Chinese brothel, at least before she "retires" as a wife at her fortieth birthday (the significance of which will be discussed later). Contrary to the stereotypical belief that "women have long tongues," Madame Wu is also "by habit a silent woman. . . . Whatever she had decided she made known in a few simple, clear words, her voice always pretty and smooth and gentle as water slipping over stones" (25).

More important, however, Madame Wu is shrewd and sagacious. She is capable of making any decision for the family and has the admirable ability to get things done the way she wants them to be done. During her twenty-two-year governance of the Wu family, her old-fashioned mother-in-law, referred to as Old Lady, is still living. Therefore, she

> had held this management in her own hands, skillfully maintaining its outward habits so that Old Lady did not notice changes, and at the same time making many changes. Thus before Madame Wu decided to do away with the overgrown peony bushes . . ., she had allowed the peonies to die one winter. When their strong red shoots did not push up as usual in the spring, she called Old Lady's attention to this and helped her to decide that peonies must have exhausted the soil and air in this garden, and therefore something else had better be planted here for a generation or two. (4)

The instances of Madame Wu's shrewdness are rampant in the novel. After Madame Wu told Liangmo, the eldest son, about her decision to arrange the marriage between Linyi and Fengmo, the third son, Liangmo expresses his doubts about whether Fengmo will let her decide for him. To this, Madame Wu replies: "If he will not, then I will let himself decide for himself to marry Linyi. . . . I never compel anyone to do anything" (82). What happens later is exactly what she promises. Later, in order to convince Linyi that Fengmo is also exposed to foreign things, Madame Wu arranges Brother André to teach Fengmo English. Fengmo does not agree, however, afraid that Brother André will try to convert him. "Do you need to yield to conversion?" Madame Wu asked. "Are you so weak? You must take from a person that which is his best and ignore all else. Come, try the priest for a month, and if you wish then to stop his teaching, I will agree to do it." Then, Buck comments: "It was the secret of her power in this house that she never allowed her will to be felt as absolute. She gave time and the promise of an end, and then she used the time to shape events to her own end" (109).

Among her four sons, Fengmo, the most ambitious and intelligent, is the most difficult to deal with. He is ready to accept new ideas, able to think his own thoughts, and does not yield easily. This offers Buck a perfect oppor-

tunity to show her heroine's shrewdness and manipulativeness. Madame
Wu knows that blind marriage does not work for Fengmo, who believes
that he, belonging to the young generation, should not marry someone without loving her. Therefore, she tries to arrange a meeting between Fengmo
and Linyi. But she also knows that Fengmo, rebellious as he is, will not
agree if she asks him directly. So she uses reverse psychology, sounding as
if she thinks that Fengmo is not interested and even lacks the courage to see
Linyi. With this, Fengmo "naturally" disagrees, insisting that he see Linyi,
thus falling into her mother's trap. There is the second trap, however, waiting for him. Madame Wu wants him to see Linyi alone. Again she knows
that he would disagree if it were a direct request or order. Then we have the
following conversation between the mother and the son:

> "Then shall I tell her mother that in a few days you and I will . . ."
> "Why you, mother?" he asked very clearly.
> "Fengmo!" she cried sharply. "I will not yield too far. How can you see
> the girl alone?"
> "Certainly I shall see her alone," Fengmo said with some anger, "Must I
> be led by my mother like a small child?"

A few turns later, Madame Wu allows Fengmo to go, reluctantly, as if she
were defeated and yielding to Fengmo's will. After Fengmo walks out of
her room to the court angrily, Madame Wu laughs and tells Ying, her maid,
who is worried because of the loud voices of the mother and son, "Oh,
nothing. . . . I wanted him to do something and he is going to do it—that is
all" (128).

Madame Wu is able to deal not only with everyone in the family—her
husband, sons, daughters-in-law—but also with anyone outside the family
who comes into contact with her—servants, shop managers, friends, and
matchmakers. When talking with Liu Ma, the matchmaker, about finding
Mr. Wu a concubine, for example, Madame Wu immediately sees through
Liu Ma's lie that she thinks Madame Wu has summoned her to find Fengmo
a wife, but she "allowed Liu Ma to think she was deceiving" (52). When it
comes to the price the Wu family will pay Chiuming's foster mother, Madame Wu offers two hundred dollars. Liu Ma wants to add fifty:

> "Let it be then," Madame Wu said so suddenly that she saw a greedy sorrow
> shine in the small old eyes that were fastened on her anxiously. "You need
> not grieve that you did not ask for more," she said. "I know what is just and
> what is generous."

To this, the defeated Liu Ma can only say: "I know your wisdom, Lady" and hurries away after a few parting words (52).

Madame Wu's dexterity and shrewdness are also seen in her ability to say the right thing to the right person at the right time. To her husband, for instance, she is clear and to the point sometimes, but ambiguous other times (33). She knows that "with a man, young or old, the important thing is the choice of time" (101) if one wants to persuade him. She has learned that "the affairs of a great household must be managed one by one and in order" (104), and that "to seem to yield is always stronger than to show resistance, and to acknowledge a fault quickly is always to show an invincible certitude" (119).

> She was careful . . . to be almost exactly the median of what she always was. That is, she was neither cold nor ardent. She was pleasant, she was tender. She saw to it that nothing was lacking, but that nothing was over and above. Fulfillment and not surfeit was her natural gift in all things. (30)

The shrewdness of Madame Wu, however, is best demonstrated in her planning and carrying out two of the major events in the novel—her arrangement of Fengmo's marriage and Mr. Wu's concubine-taking.

While it is Madame Wu's responsibility to arrange marriages for her son, and she has done it in good faith, her motivation for finding a wife for Fengmo is not a usual one. When she summons Chiuming to the house for the first time, Fengmo accidentally runs into her. This causes Madame Wu enough alarm: "Who could tell what fire would blaze out of this" (73)? To prevent a possible disturbance in the family, she immediately decides to betroth Fengmo.

There is a problem, however. Since Linyi has been to school, she will demand that her husband be able to speak a foreign language. But to send Fengmo to school to learn a foreign language would be too radical for Madame Wu. Therefore, she decides to hire a tutor, Brother André, to teach Fengmo, without telling Fengmo the real motive. When Brother André comes to the house, Madame Wu sternly stipulates that he is to teach "only the language" (117), for "to teach a mind is to assume the power over it" (118).

In her arrangement of a concubine for her husband, we see more of Madame Wu's shrewdness. Since, as she well knows, such a decision will create an uproar in the family, she has to explain why she has so decided. She tells different people different reasons. To Liangmo, the eldest son, who is the first one to hear the news, she says that "It is because I have always been happy with your father, and he with me, that I have decided on the step" (16). To Mr. Wu, she gives two reasons: the biological difference between men and women, such that for a woman, at the age of forty, half of her life is over, but for a man, his half is still far away (31), and that "It looks very ill for a woman over fifty to bear a child" (32). To her friend, Madame Kang, who begs for explanation, she refuses to say anything and skillfully changes the topic of conversation (98). Only to Rulan, her second daughter-in-law, she says, "I will spend the rest of my life assembling my mind and my own soul" (47), which is a little closer to the truth.

When it comes to the choosing of the concubine, Madame Wu specifically requires that she be:

> A pretty woman, . . . very pretty but not beautiful. A girl—a woman, that is—about twenty-two years old, round-cheeked and young and soft as a child, ready in her affection to love anybody and not just one man—someone who does not, indeed, love too deeply any man, and who will, for a new coat or a sweet, forget a trouble—who loves children, of course, good-tempered—and whose family is far away so that she will not be always crying for home—. (55)

This "job description" has taken much thinking of Madame Wu. Every requirement is purposeful. Clearly, she wants someone who can function well in the Wu family and who will not create the kind of turbulence she is painfully aware of.

A few days later, the chosen girl comes to Madame Wu. After carefully inspecting her—her breath, teeth, hands, neck, face, and dress—and conversing with her about her background, she lets the girl sleep in her sitting room for a few nights

> until the girl understood her place in the family and until she, too, understood the girl. There must be some deep accord established between them before she released her from this court to enter the other, else trouble might arise in the house. She was doing a delicate and difficult thing, and it must be done skillfully. (68)

So, peace in the house is Madame Wu's priority of the concubine-taking event, not the happiness of these two involved. There are good reasons for this. First, in a traditional Chinese family, particularly one of high social status like the Wu's, peace was of paramount importance, for disturbances of any kind would be viewed as scandals, thus damaging the family reputation. Second, marriage was not considered the result of love. Rather, it was regarded as a necessity through arrangement.

Madame Wu's shrewdness is seen not only in the actual handling of the family matters but also in the fact that she does not step over boundaries of the Confucian codes. It is true that it is highly unusual for a wife to offer to find a concubine for her husband, but concubinage is perfectly in line with the social practices at the time. It is true that she arranges the marriage between Fengmo and Linyi, not for their happiness but for freeing herself one step further, but society dictates that parents are to decide their children's marriages.

Madame Wu also enjoys the utmost trust and respect of all in the household. Her eldest son, Liangmo, "trusted her wisdom far more than he did his own." When she asks him to marry, he says: "Choose someone for me, mother. You know me better than I know myself" (15). In the Wu family, "She made all decisions" (25) and whatever she says is final. Her role in the family is summarized well by Ying, her servant, "in this great house all feed on her, like sucking children" (48).

To fully understand Madame Wu as a literary character as well as a Chinese woman, however, we need to go beyond what she does and into what she is. Her greatest individuality is, perhaps, that in her we see both intuition, which is supposedly more of a trait in women, and intelligence, which has been prejudicially ascribed only to men. Thus, Madame Wu is not a woman, but a combination of man and woman.

There is no lack of instances in the novel that testify to Madame Wu's intuition and perceptiveness. When observing the soon-to-be concubine, Chiuming, she sees her undevelopedness in her face, her intelligence in her eyes, and her possible origin from a piece of cloth that was once used to wrap her when she was discarded by her parents. As indicated earlier, she senses that trouble might come out of Fengmo's and Chiuming's seeing each other, and trouble does come later in the book when Chiuming tells her that she has been furtively in love with Fengmo. In a word, she can always see the minds of anybody and anticipate what he/she will say or do, through his or her facial expressions, words, and even bodily movements.

Madame Wu's intelligence is primarily seen in her relentless pursuit of freedom and internal peace. Her father-in-law, a scholar and high government official, discovers her intelligence soon after she comes into the Wu family at the age of eighteen. He tells Madame Wu: "We chose you for our son because you were beautiful and good and because your grandfather was the former viceroy of this province. Now I find that you are also intelligent" (60). "Your mind is an excellent one for a woman. . . . I would even say, my daughter, that had your brain been inside the skull of a man, you would have sat for the Imperial Examinations and passed them with honor and become thereby an official in the land" (59–60).

Unfortunately, intelligence was not something that a woman was supposed to possess. When Madame Wu is very young, her father-in-law forbids her from reading some of his books because "men love women when they are not too knowing" (62). He also believes that Madame Wu is so beautiful that she does not need a brain also (60). It is here that we have the first glimpse of the oppression Madame Wu faces. Women were sex objects for men: As long as they were beautiful, they did not need anything else.

Partly, at least, because of her intelligence, Madame Wu is never satisfied with what she has as the First Lady in a very rich, powerful, and well-respected family. Instead, she has, since a very early age, been dreaming of and planning for the day when she will be free. She does not cherish the power and status resulting from mother-in-lawhood as traditional women would. Rather, she views such power and respect as a hurdle on her way to spiritual freedom. Therefore she decides to give up the power, retiring at the age of forty. Furthermore, unlike other women of her time who sought happiness in giving birth to boys and in being able to please their husbands, Madame Wu treats these two things as no more than burdens. The birth of a child

> was not birth so much as reclaiming her own body. Her first thought when the pain stopped abruptly and when she heard that sharp cry of the separate child was always of her own freedom. As soon as the child was brought to her, washed and dressed, she began to love him for what he was, but never because he was part of herself. She did not, indeed, wish for any division of herself. She wanted only to be whole again. (93)

Neither does Madame Wu think that marriage is part of a woman's happiness. It is only a duty. Therefore, not long after her wedding with Mr. Wu, she begins to look forward to her fortieth birthday. When she is separated from Mr. Wu and finds out that she has never loved him, she feels as if "the last chain fell from her soul. Time and again she had picked up those chains and put them on. But now no more. There was no need. She was wholly free of him " (140).

Thus, to Madame Wu, love itself is a burden as well. She seems to think that love is mundane, something that hinders her pursuit of internal peace. If one wants to gain spiritual freedom, one cannot be bound to any earthly ties, be they material, social, emotional, or sexual.

For one who does not allow herself to be contented with earthly happiness, she is bound to feel lonely, separated from others. This is the very problem Madame Wu faces:

> She did not know she was lonely, and had anyone told her that she was, she would have denied it, amazed at such misreading. But she was too lonely for anyone to reach her soul. Her soul had outstripped her life. It had gone out far beyond the four walls within which her body lived. It roamed the world, and reached into past and climbed the future, and her many thoughts played about that constant voyaging. (110)

At one time, "She was suddenly so lonely. . . . She stood on top of a peak, surrounded by ice and cold, lost and solitary. She wanted to cry out, but her voice would not come from her throat" (125).

The lonely Madame Wu is not lonely only. Standing "on top of a peak," she is aloof; she is superior; she is arrogant. It is here that we see the greatest individuality of Madame Wu as a character: she is lonely because she is traveling a road on which there are few travelers; she is aloof because she values spirituality while others do not; she is arrogant because she looks at her fellow beings with disdain. She tells Fengmo that "I am not a fool, though all the world around me are fools" (108). She dislikes everyone around her:

> Thus her mother she had disliked because of her ignorance and superstitions. Her father she had loved, or would have said she had, but she had disliked him, too, because his heart was far away and she could never come near him. And though Mr. Wu had been a handsome young man when she married him there were secrets of his person which she disliked. Even when she had shared his passion, she had been aware of shapes and odors, and she had felt violation in his touch even while she allowed it. Old Gentleman had been dear to her, but she was so delicately made that she could not forget what she disliked while she found what she liked. His heart was good, his intelligence clear, but his teeth were broken and his breath came foul. (225)

Here, Buck seems to suggest that the mind and the body are one. While Madame Wu strives to achieve spirituality, she is conscious of her bodily wholeness. Physical contact with others, disagreeable sight of others' body parts, and the presence of others' ignorance are all viewed as invasions of her own purity, both physical and spiritual.

More importantly, Madame Wu does not only have the yearning for freedom, but also the courage to act so as to gain freedom. She is fully aware that society has put on women all kinds of responsibilities and chains. She cannot be free until she has successfully fulfilled these responsibilities and shaken off these chains. As a result, she has performed wonderfully in the Wu family: she has given birth to three sons, although she does not want to divide herself again and again. She uses all her wisdom and shrewdness to arrange the sons' marriages, and after each arrangement, she feels more complete and free. She has always wanted to be free of her husband, but she makes efforts to be a good wife:

> She had been careful to keep him satisfied in all things. Did he feel a desire for knowledge concerning any matter to be found in books, she informed herself and then told him. Did he mention a curiosity concerning foreign things, she learned and let him know. In all their years he had not an unsatisfied desire. But she knew without pain that this was because she had studied his wishes and when they were vague, by careful discourse she helped them to emerge clearly, even to himself, and when they were sharp and immediate she wasted no time to satisfy him. (74)

The oppression Madame Wu experiences is clearly seen here: as a Chinese woman, she has to sacrifice much to obtain what she wants. While she intends to pursue freedom from an early age, she has to devote twenty-two years of her life to the family before she begins the endeavor. While this injustice might not be as apparent to the reader as more observable injustices would be, such as having to wait upon the husband and the in-laws and not being allowed to marry after the husband is dead, it is in no way less tolerable or more justifiable: Why does a woman have to sacrifice twenty-two years of her life for something that she is entitled to in the first place?

To make this woman's struggle for freedom more difficult, Madame Wu's sacrifice turns out futile: after her long-awaited fortieth birthday, she finds out that she is not free at all. First, Fengmo does not love Linyi because he cannot find understanding and companionship in her. Second, Tsemo does not love Rulan because Rulan is years older than he is and does not know how to please him despite all her efforts. Third, and most importantly, Mr. Wu is not contented with Chiuming; neither is she with him. Therefore, Mr. Wu has begun to frequent flower houses, for he thinks that "it is easier simply to buy women without expecting them to love" (191). Madame Wu finds out from all this that she might never be truly free:

> "Oh, Heaven." Madame Wu cried in a sort of strange agony, "am I to be responsible forever for him [Mr. Wu]?"

She felt the wings of her soul, poised and widespread, now droop and falter earthward again. (193)

Perhaps, in Chinese society at the time, a woman was not destined to gain freedom. She was chained by all kinds of earthly responsibilities, which, however hard she tries, would never be fulfilled. This oppression is the oppression in its extreme form. It is the kind of oppression that only women like Madame Wu faced. Other women's longing for freedom had perhaps been smothered by society before it ever took shape.

To shake off this chain, obviously, the Chinese woman needs something else, something that society does not provide. Madame Wu is lucky, for this something eventually comes to her, though accidentally. It is Brother André.

Brother André is a Western white man, although he claims to have no country, no name ("André" has been given to him), and he does not remember his parents. Neither does he know what his religion is. He speaks many languages "in order to converse with all people" (115). On their first meeting, he discerns that Madame Wu is not happy, which "struck Madame Wu as sharply as though a hidden knife had pierced her without knowing exactly where it had struck" (116). He insists on taking no fee for teaching Fengmo English, for he believes that religion is better without money (116). All this arouses in Madame Wu a curiosity, making her feel that Brother André is here to present her another world. From then on, she seizes every opportunity to talk to him when he comes to teach Fengmo.

Brother André is, to Madame Wu, who has been confined to the Wu family all her life, full of new, outlandish ideas. He explains that his religion is in everyday life activities, like eating, sleeping, walking, working, and helping others. He believes that "there is no difference between one blood and another" (153). And his faith is in space and in emptiness, in suns and stars, clouds and winds" (154). During their many conversations, he told Madame Wu everything he knows:

He told her the history of the world, the rise of people and their fall, the birth of new nations. He told her of the discovery of electricity and of radium; he explained to her the waves of the air which carry man's words and his music around the world. (187)

From all these new ideas and knowledge, Madame Wu's thirst for spiritual pursuit is gradually satisfied. She is going beyond the four walls of the Wu household. The Wu family, the city, even the nation, is a small part of the world, which is, in turn, only one of the numerous members of the universe. She realizes the shortness of life and the insignificance of the Wu family. At one time, while her mind travels through history and in the universe, she goes into a trance, which causes a family disturbance as they think that her soul has fled her (155).

However, the expansion of her horizon does not directly translate into freedom, and Madame Wu cannot simply think of stars and the world in her trance all her life. There are problems to be solved. For Madame Wu, she must find out what she has done wrong to have caused these problems. About Mr. Wu's concubine-taking, Brother André tells Madame Wu that she has mistakenly considered her husband entirely flesh and has "bought a young woman as you would buy a pound of pork" (200). As a result, he points out, Madame Wu has been guilty of three sins:

> You have despised your husband, you have held in contempt a sister woman, and you have considered yourself unique and above all women. These sins have disturbed your house. Without knowing why, your sons have been restless and their wives unhappy, and in spite of your plans no one is happy. (200)

Such blunt accusations would not work if the accused refuses to admit her mistakes. Madame Wu is not such a person. She gradually realizes her mistakes. She becomes conscious that "She had made herself a prisoner inside the confines of her will, imposed upon her body" (223). When Chiuming tells her that she has been in love with Fengmo, she blames herself for this "fruit of her stupidity, without love" (246). When Tsemo dies, she realizes that "she had known him only as a son, hers because she had made his flesh, but not because she had become acquainted with his being" (285). To all the family,

> What she had done so selfishly was to try to free herself from them all by withdrawing herself. She had wanted them to be happy, each in his own fashion, but she had not wanted to be troubled with making them happy, nor had she been able to tell them how to be happy. Food and clothing she had provided, discipline and order she had maintained, and yet the whole house was in a turmoil and nobody was happy. She had been angry with them because they were not happy. This she now saw was completely foolish. (219)

Here we see another admirable quality of Madame Wu: she is ready to admit mistakes. While Madame Wu can blame herself for not thinking about others' happiness first, others, both those in the novel and the readers of the novel, cannot accuse her, for she has done all these things with good faith and in line with the social practices at the time. A women with less intelligence who does not pursue spiritual freedom will perhaps not admit that these things are wrong doings. By this, Buck places Madame Wu at a higher spiritual level than her peers.

But what can Madame Wu do to remedy her wrongdoing? André says she should forget her own self. Rather than thinking about her freedom all the time, she should think about freeing others from her. From this guidance comes Madame Wu's greatest realization:

> Nothing, she reflected, was as easy as she had thought. Freedom was not a matter of arrangement. She had seen freedom hanging like a peach from a tree. She had nurtured the tree, and when it bore she had seized upon the fruit and found it green. (201)

Madame Wu thus realizes that freedom cannot be gotten at the expense of others. She cannot free herself until she frees others.

Once she realizes her mistakes, Madame Wu does not hesitate to correct them. Thus, she lets Fengmo "go free" to a foreign country, and has Brother André to teach Linyi so as to shorten the distance between the couple. She also sends Tsemo away and prepares Rulan, with all her wisdom, to gain Tsemo's love. To Chiuming, her admission of mistake is direct:

> It has been shown me that I did you a great wrong, my sister. It is true that you were brought here as I might have bought a pound of pork. How could I dare so to behave towards a human being? I see now that I had no thought for your soul. (202)

Madame Wu also tells Mr. Wu that she has been "very selfish" and now she sees her "wrong" (204). She offers to send Chiuming away and herself go back to Mr. Wu, because she realizes that "she could never be free until she had offered herself up utterly" (204). In other words, she realizes that as a wife, she has the responsibility to offer her husband happiness, a responsibility that she has to fulfill before she can think of her own needs. However, Mr. Wu has found love in Jasmine and rejects her offer. He says he wants to buy Jasmine out and put her in a separate house. This time, truly with Mr. Wu's happiness in mind, she tells Mr. Wu to let Jasmine live under his own roof.

Another daring deed of Madame Wu is to take the orphans—more than twenty in number—left by André when he dies to the Wu family to be fed, raised, and educated. She does this not only because it is Andre's will, but also because she has been enlightened to place the freedom of others above the freedom of her own.

The changes in Madame Wu do not stop at what she does for others. More profound changes are felt in her mind, and, almost mystically, in her body. She is "coming to some sort of secret exquisite bloom. She met each day with relish and joy" (186). When she wakes up every morning, "she was aware of fresh energy in herself" (217). Her maid, Ying, remarks that her "skin is rosy as a child's" (224). After Brother André dies, Madame Wu very often reflects on the many conversations she has had with him. She will use what he told her to solve her problems. She notices that "The springs of my being are different. I shall no longer live out of duty but out of love" (215). "She now realized that for the first time in her life she disliked no one. All her life she had struggled against her dislike of human beings. None has been wholly to her taste" (225). Love "descended as the sunshine did and the rain, upon just and unjust alike, upon rich and poor, upon the ignorant and the learned . . ." (229). How about the old way of love and marriage through arrangement, then? Perhaps it is wrong, she concludes (300).

Because of love, Madame Wu's attitude towards others also changes. When she decides to take Andre's orphans home, she says "there is room here for all," which deeply touches Ying, making her so happy that she begins to cry, sobbing: "You're changed—you are changed" (226). Later when she goes to see these children, they surround her and she smiles and receives their welcome, not putting them away from her, although "she had often shrunk from the touch of her own children when they were small, and she had sometimes disliked even their hands upon her" (276). When Tsemo dies, she tells Fengmo that she will help Rulan, the widow, to remarry if she so chooses. When Fengmo tells her about his parting from a foreign girl he loves, Madame Wu says: "What sorrow, my son" (286). The understanding amazes Fengmo.

Love makes Madame Wu change, love helps her gain freedom, love renders the family happy. Madame Wu not only allows Jasmine into the house, but also gives her the title of the Third Lady. Mr. Wu stops visiting flower houses and the two live in love and happiness. As for Chiuming, she sends her to care for the orphans, until later her biological mother finds her and takes her away, an action to which Madame Wu readily agrees. Years later, Chiuming gets happily married.

Madame Wu also tries hard to remedy the marriages of her two sons, Tsemo and Fengmo. She tells Rulan all she has learned from Brother André and her own thinking, teaching her how to love, how to perform duty, and, most importantly, how to separate the two. She also sends Ying to help Rulan to make up, for Rulan is one who "cares nothing for her beauty" (258). Thus when Tsemo comes home from the capital, the couple find their love for the first time and live happily for ten days until Tsemo dies in a plane crash when he is leaving home.

The next year, Fengmo comes home from America. He will never love Linyi, Madame Wu realizes, but he finds his happiness in providing schools for farmers and becomes a very successful educator. Rulan and Linyi become teachers for him, and they all work, in happiness, to free others.

The twenty or so orphans also end up in happiness. They are so well brought up that it becomes an honor for young men to marry them. Every one of them is married to a good family and becomes a good wife.

Looking at the long path Madame Wu takes to her freedom and internal peace, one might think that she would never achieve her ends without Brother André. However, this judgment can be a mistake. As Brother André admits, he has attempted to enlighten others, but he teaches Madame Wu as he has "never taught another," because:

> It was so pellucid a soul, so wise and yet so young. She had lived in this house and had learned so much through her own living that she was ripe with understanding. Her mind was a crystal cup, the workmanship complete, the cup only waiting to be filled. (187)

Here we see in Madame Wu a soul that is ready to be edified and enlightened. Without this readiness, Brother Andre's teaching would have come to no avail. To use a metaphor from Mao, a hen can hatch chickens out of eggs, but not egglike pebbles.

Another misconception a reader might have is that Madame Wu's freedom is a triumph of Christianity. It is true that Brother André is from the Christian tradition, for he makes frequent references to Christ, the Garden of Eden, and calls his foundlings "lambs." But he is, Madame Wu later learns from his nephew, a heretic compelled from his homeland by his own religion. What Brother André has taught Madame Wu is not Christianity, but love. "Gods she [Madame Wu] did not worship, and faith she had none, but love she had and for ever" (316).

Madame Wu's freedom is therefore a freedom gained in a Chinese context. In such a context, freedom requires much from a woman. She has to be unique in character; she has to have intelligence and ability; and, above all, she has to free all others until she can free herself. The difficulty involved in such an attempt is well illustrated by Madame Wu's desperate realization, during her struggle toward freedom, that women have no gods: while men can find gods, "For women true gods were impossible. . . . The women whom she knew best and had known best in her whole life, not one of them had truly sought God" (214).[1]

In this unique Chinese context, Madame Wu stands out as a highly individualized character. Her intelligence and ability are a challenge to the Confucian doctrine that "a woman's virtue is her lack of knowledge." The combination of her beauty and intelligence runs counter to the stereotypical image of women that they are less smart than men. Her actions, after she is enlightened by Brother André, such as allowing Jasmine to be the Third Lady, promising to help Rulan remarry if she so chooses, and taking Andre's foundlings home to rear, made her unique among those in her position. She eventually gains freedom and internal peace, something that few Chinese women at her time were able to accomplish.

Madame Wu's individuality becomes even clearer when we compare her to other characters. Her lifelong friend, Madame Kang, for example, is also pretty, well brought up, and is the First Lady in the Kang family, which is as rich and important as the Wu family, but she is much less intelligent and capable. Her household is badly managed—the children are rowdy and difficult, the servants are badly behaved, and the house is always dirty and messy. The maids even hold the children to urinate in front of guests. Mr. Kang has been frequenting flower houses all his life, but Madame Kang considers it usual and thinks nothing of it. She views her life as having no meaning but to please her husband and bear him children.

Meng, Madame Kang's daughter and Madame Wu's first daughter-in-law, offers us another comparison to Madame Wu. She thinks her husband such a good man that

> [s]he found no fault with him. She was lost in him and content to be lost. She wanted no being of her own. To be his, to lie in his arms at nights, to serve him by day, to fold his garments, to bring his food herself, pour his tea and light his pipe, to hasten to his every word, to busy herself with healing any slight headache, to test the flavor of a dish or the heat of the wine, these were her joys and her occupations. But above all was the bearing of his children. To bear him many children was her sole desire. She was his instrument for immortality. (49)

Even when, at the end of the novel, Fengmo asks her to help him with his work of educating farmers' children, Meng not only refuses, but also thinks that Fengmo is leading Rulan and Linyi astray. She goes to tell on Fengmo to Madame Wu, and Madame Wu has to issue an order to Fengmo not to bother Meng anymore.

Individuality and typicality, however, are dependent upon each other. If a protagonist is entirely a type character, she becomes flat. If she is too individualized, she may lose her credibility. Buck knew this well and has therefore given Madame Wu qualities typical of women of her times.

In the Wu family, Madame Wu "steadfastly followed the one [old custom] which separated male from female at an early age" (72). She has separated her sons from all women at the age of seven. Before her enlightenment from André, she believes that a son should not be allowed into society before he is shaped (83). When her mother-in-law dies, she thinks of calling André for funeral services, but decides to follow the old ways to call Chinese Buddhist monks (142). Later in the novel, Fengmo comes home and tells the family that there are Chinese in America who wash clothes for a living. Madame Wu claims, "Certainly our people ought not to wash the soiled garments of foreigners" (291). Madame Wu's individuality therefore stems from her typicality. In her we see Buck's dexterity in characterization—a combination of uniqueness and credibility.

If we move from Madame Wu the heroine to Buck the novelist, we find that she deeply sympathizes with her Chinese women characters, loves them, and condemns, with her powerful pen, the unfair treatment they have received for thousands of years. Through Madame Wu, she drives home the nature of oppression man has exercised upon women:

> Had she not created even him? Perhaps for that he never forgave her, but hated her and fought her secretly, and dominated her and oppressed her and kept her locked in house and her feet bound and her waist tied, and forbade her wages and skills and learning, and widowed her when he was dead, and burned her sometimes to ashes, pretending that it was her faithfulness that did it. (249)

These few lines succinctly summarize the conditions of Chinese women throughout history. They represent women's awareness of such conditions and their challenge to and rebellion against them.

However, this awareness is not possessed by all women. In fact, most women, as represented by Kwei-lan's mother in *East Wind: West Wind*, are so much conditioned by the Confucian doctrines and social forces that they have never realized the injustice in those social practices and, therefore, have become instruments to maintain and perpetuate such practices.

Buck's sympathy toward Chinese women can also be seen in her narration. When Chiuming, the concubine, speaks of her first night with Mr. Wu, we read:

> He smiled, and his smooth handsome face lit from a sudden heat from within him. She saw it and understood it. But tonight she would not be afraid. It was a little price to pay, a very little price to pay a kind man, for a home at last. (112)

This time, instead of open rebellion, Buck shows her indignation in the silent way the character yields to the strong societal power. She tells her reader, through her subdued, yet protesting narration, that "Look, you men! You make us women pay for a roof to live under with our bodies and souls."

As if this is not enough, Buck portrays her female characters as far superior to male characters in almost every way. Take Mr. Wu for example. He has been spoiled, is incapable, knows nothing, and has no interest in learning and thinking. He leaves everything to Madame Wu and concerns himself only with his material comfort and sexual pleasure. He adores Madame Wu while she is disgusted with him, feeling "violation in his touch even while she allows it" (225). Throughout the novel, he is no more than a shadow, always remaining in the background, coming to the foreground only when there are problems. As a result,

> Whatever Madame Wu had fostered in him had faded away, like a light dimmed because it fed on no fuel. He grew gross and heavy, eating too much and drinking often but always with Jasmine. . . . There in the court where they lived so closely together that almost they lived alone, they were ribald and gay and drunken and happy, two pieces of meat and bone, and content so to be. The name of Mr. Wu was seldom heard now even in his own house. In malice a servant whispered it to another, and that was all. (293)

As noted by critics, Buck's female characters are almost always better than male characters. This might offend male readership, particularly a Chinese male. But perhaps Buck does this for a purpose: because the unfair treatment of Chinese women has been deeply rooted, she intended to exceed the proper limits to correct it.

To summarize, we find Madame Wu a highly individualized character. In fact, she is the most individualized of all characters studied in this book. In crafting such a complicated, multidimensional character, Buck places Madame Wu among the finest women characters in literature. Madame Wu the Chinese woman is "immortal" (316) because she has found love and gained her spiritual freedom. Madame Wu the character is immortal because Buck has put all her love and craftsmanship into the portrayal of her.

4

Servant Women in *Peony*

P_{EONY} DESERVES SPECIAL ATTENTION FOR TWO REASONS. FIRST, UNLIKE OTHER novels dealt with in this book whose heroines are wives in various types of Chinese families (although Kwei-lan in *East Wind: West Wind* goes through a process of becoming a wife), Peony is a single woman working as a servant in a Jewish family. As discussed in chapter 2, at the time—about mid-nineteenth century—when the story took place, women had no place in society and were not allowed to work outside the family by themselves. Working as servants in rich families became the most common occupation single women—usually from poor families—could find to make a living. Therefore, the analysis of Peony can shed light on the situation of single women: how they as servants were oppressed by society and how they acted to cope with such oppression. Second, dealing with the interracial relationship between the Chinese and the Jews, *Peony* is one of a kind among Buck's novels. From it we can detect Buck's view of the Chinese attitude toward and treatment of other people.

The following discussion will show that, first, women servants in China were even more oppressed than women of other social status. Life offered them very little indeed, and, as a result, they had to struggle even harder and resort to underground ways in order to obtain what they thought they deserved. Second, in terms of characterization, Buck presents Peony as more of a typical character than an individualized one, a representative of the Chinese people when they come into contact with a different race.

Before getting into the analysis of characterization, it is necessary to discuss in some detail the theme of the novel, and Buck's inconsistent perspectives of how the Chinese view and treat other peoples.

In "Wings," accompanying *Peony*, Buck (1948a) says that the idea of writing *Peony* first came to her "as a question: What is the source of human understanding that lies so deep in the heart of all Chinese?" She later explains the reason:

from the earliest times the Chinese sages and philosophers and priests have
had the vision of the humanity . . . that all men are brothers. The humblest
peasant in China has been taught this belief by his humble parents, and the
commonest words upon his tongue are the proverbs, that heaven is above
and earth beneath us all, that all under Heaven are one family, that if there is
anything that he does not like done to him, he must not do to another. . . . (7)

No matter how well-meaning Buck might have been, however, there are
several problems in her views. First, although it is true that "Under the sun
all are brothers" is one of the numerous sayings of the Chinese, it is not
clear that this saying has been transformed into practice. The Chinese have
been known to view themselves as the center of the earth, the idea of which
is reflected even in the name of the country: *Zhongguo* (China) literally
means "Middle Kingdom." And they called almost any other people "barbarians" or "foreign devils."

Even if we suppose that Chinese people viewed other people as equals
as Buck seems to believe, we still see two inconsistencies in Buck's characters. First, on the one hand, Peony claims to respect the Jews; on the
other, she tries to steer the Ezra family away from their own tradition toward the life of the Chinese. The reason for this can only be arrogance: the
Chinese appear to believe that their way of life is a better alternative to
happiness. Second, there are ample instances in Buck's works that the Chinese view other people as anything but equal: Kwei-lan's mother in *East
Wind: West Wind* refuses, until her death, to recognize the American woman
as daughter-in-law, and even the open-minded Madame Wu has feelings
against the "barbarians."

The third problem is that Buck does not seem to realize the implication
of the efforts by the Chinese to help the Jewish people assimilate into the
Chinese way of life. To Buck, assimilation is not a loss of identity, but
identity kept in a different form. "Their spirit is born anew in every generation. They are no more and yet they are forever" (*Peony*, 312). But to those
who were assimilated, assimilation is a loss of identity and an extinction of
culture. This is perhaps something any people would fear, let alone the
Jews, who have known cruel persecution too well.

After *Peony* was published in 1948, many Jews wrote to Buck, express-
ing their horror at the idea of assimilation and their opinion that the persecution they had suffered was not solely because of their belief that they
were the chosen people. Besides, their insistence on remaining a separate
people had other reasons—mostly emotional. To this, Buck first argued
that she had only recorded the fact of what happened to the Jews in China,

but later responded to their criticism apologetically, admitting that she was, in a way, "naive" when she wrote *Peony* (Harris 1969, 2:42).

On the other hand, however, Buck is right in her observation that the kind of racial problems that have plagued the Western world have never bothered China. This is, it seems, not because the Chinese treat other people as equals without any prejudice, but because, maintaining that their way of life is better, the Chinese, consciously or unconsciously, have assimilated them, gradually melting them into their own culture. The difference between the young West and the old East does not appear to be that "the Westerner feels himself unique and the Easterner feels himself one of the human race" (Buck 1948a, 1), but that the Westerner considers himself unique, thus rejecting others, while the Easterner, particularly the Chinese, considers himself superior and powerful, thus welcoming others to change their way of life to fit into his own. Such a feeling of superiority is not hard to understand: as a world leader for centuries, the Chinese seem to have formed in them an unfortunate self-deceiving arrogance. Beginning from the nineteenth century, when they found themselves behind others, particularly in science and technology, the Chinese have refused to believe that they are no longer the "Middle Kingdom," the center of the world, let alone admit it.

Buck is also right in that the Chinese people have "warmth" and are able to be tolerant. They may feel superior, but they are "willing to accept them [the Jews] wholly into their bloodstream. The Jews there could not remain a separate people because the warm life of the Chinese absorbs them" (1). There is also evidence for this in history. During the two thousand years of feudalism, many minorities conquered the Han and ruled the country for centuries. The Mongolians, for example, established the Yuan Dynasty (1277–1367) and the Man people were the last feudal rulers in the Qing Dynasty (1644–1911).[1] These rulers, however, found themselves gradually losing their own tradition and yielding to that of the Han, thus getting totally submerged in the Han culture.[2]

Warmth is an important aspect of Chinese culture (Gu 1990). To show warmth is to be polite and to care. Therefore, many Chinese ways of social interaction would seem imposing to the Westerner. If I, a Chinese, see you, a Western guest in my house, dressed too thinly for the weather, I will urge you to put on more clothes or simply "force" you to accept a jacket when you go out into the cold. You might think my behavior downright imposing, impolite or rude, but to me it is a way of showing care and politeness. I have experienced such embarrassment from an American woman who burst into a rage— "How can you tell me how to live my life?"—when I indicated that she might be wearing too little in the cold weather of Xi'an.

Despite the problems Buck faces, *Peony* as a novel has merits: It is based on the historical fact that Jews have merged into the Chinese civilization. Her characterization of Peony helps explain why this has happened. However, the reader should keep the above problems in mind so that the following analysis can be put in perspective.

During Buck's time in China, having bondmaids was a common practice in rich families. Bondmaids usually came very young, because their parents thought that sending them to a rich family was a better alternative than having them starved. As bondmaids, they occupied a special position in the family:

> If they enter the average well-to-do home, it is as something more than a servant, although less than a daughter. It is their task to serve, even in childish ways, and as they grow older, they may, if they have beauty and intelligence, become very powerful indeed in the family. Their duty is to make life more pleasant for everybody and if they are good, as Peony was, they do this duty. (Buck 1948a, 6)

Since bondmaids usually grew up with their young male masters, very often there would develop a close relationship between them—something a little short of a brother-and-sister relationship.

This special position had two implications. First, if the bondmaids were pretty and well behaved, they could gain warmth and affection from the family, be well provided for materially, and pick up some education while serving the masters during their lessons. Second, they have the right to be married, not to sons of the family, but to some upper servants, farmers, or small merchants. This right, however, was refused by Peony, because she could not marry any other man while she loved her young master David.

As for the warmth and affection bondmaids received from their masters' family, there were limits: They were servants after all, and the Chinese tradition did not allow them to be equals with other members of the family. For one thing, they were to obey their masters and were not allowed to talk back. Therefore, their power strictly lay within the limit of obedience. This is summarized well by Wang Ma, an older servant in the novel, who used to be a bondmaid when young: "Obey—obey—and do what you like. The two go together—if you are clever" (56). Here we see a paradox: How can one do what she wants and obey the masters at the same time? However, this paradox is more apparent than real: Obedience offered love, respect, and power, which could translate into a greater possibility to maneuver, making it easier to "Do what you want." This is exactly what Peony does.

As a character, Peony strikes the reader as a typical bondmaid. She is bought into the Ezra family as a companion as well as a servant for the solitary child David. Though one is master and the other bondmaid, David and Peony grow up like brother and sister who have shared both their happiness and sorrows, their little thoughts and secrets.

Peony is beautiful and delicate in appearance and faithful and capable in her duties. She knows all the rites of the sacred days in the Jewish tradition (2). She takes it as her responsibility that everything in the house is properly run according to the wishes of the masters.

During the years, she has learned the proper behavior as suited for her position as a bondmaid. It is through her behavior that we have the first glimpse of her position in the family. She knows "perfectly how to sit at ease, waiting, her look pleasant and yielding. There was no impatience or urgency in her bearing" (35). When the master and mistress are present, she remains "properly silent" (1), stands, often behind the master and mistress, "quietly watchful" (2), and is always ready to take commands and serve. If she needs to, she speaks in her sweet, soft, and "small pretty voice" (65) and moves around the house noiselessly and gracefully. She has learned to reduce her presence in the house and tries to please the family in whatever way she can.

She has also learned to hide her own feelings, allowing herself only "the smallest of smiles" (24). Though she loves David, she shows no sign of hurt upon seeing the intimacy between David and Leah and hearing her master and mistress talking about David's marriage in front of her. All she can do is to force "a sweet fixed smile" upon her lips while busying herself (8) with housework, because she knows too well that a servant's feelings are irrelevant in the family. They are to be smothered by herself and ignored by others.

As a servant, therefore, Peony is more oppressed than the women characters in other novels, such as Madame Wu, Kwei-lan, the mother, and O-lan, all wives in their respective families. Because of her personality, behavior, and competence, however, Peony has won love and trust from the Ezra family. "If she were not in the mainstream of its warmth and affection, yet the abundance of both overflowed upon her" (9). "She had felt almost a daughter in the house. . . ." (33).

Peony is intelligent, too. Since one of her responsibilities is to attend David and his tutor, Peony has learned to read and write over the years.

"This learning, added to her own graceful talent, had made her able to turn a verse as well as David could himself" (*Peony*, 30). In fact, she has mastered the knowledge even better than David:

> Peony had read many books, and Ezra had allowed her to talk with him sometimes, and she had listened long hours to the old Confucian Chinese teacher while she was teaching David. . . . Peony had *guided* David into his love of music and poetry making, and they had read together in secret such books as *The Dream of the Red Chamber.* . . . (81; emphasis mine)

Buck's effort in portraying Peony as intelligent, good, and beautiful makes Peony a lovely character, but we do not see her as a highly individualized character, at least not yet. Being born into humble families and brought into rich ones does not necessarily mean that these bondmaids would be plain-looking and less intelligent. In fact, as portrayed in Chinese literary works and films, many bondmaids are beautiful and intelligent.

All these set the stage for the most important event in the novel: Peony's love affair with David. Through this affair, we see the fate of a bondmaid: the fact that she could not marry the one she loves, and, being a single woman servant, she has no family of her own to turn to for support or comfort. It is also here that we see how Peony has to rely solely on herself and exercise her limited power to obtain the next best thing while the best is out of reach.

Since the young masters were the ones with whom bondmaids had the closest contacts and upon whom they depended, it was only natural for bondmaids to fall in love with their masters. This is exactly what happens to Peony. David has been all her world since childhood. She knows David better than his parents, has shared his mind and thought, and has been comforted by him. For instance, when she weeps over the sad stories she and David read together in secret, "David had put his arm about her that she might weep against his shoulder" (82). As a bondmaid, however, she cannot even dream to be David's wife, for the social gap between them is too wide to cross. In such situations, the love stories usually end in tragedies, and Peony knows this well.

In fact, Peony cannot show her affection towards David, for "If ever she [Madame Ezra] saw proof that there was more between David and Peony than there should be between a young man and a serving maid, that day she would marry Peony to a farmer" (32).

Arguably, to love, to express love, and to pursue marriage based on love are among the most basic rights for a human being, but none of these belonged to a Chinese bondmaid at the time. From this we see the oppression of bondmaids by society and the hypocrisy of the society's attitudes toward bondmaids: Although they may be loved and respected to a certain degree, when it comes to marriage, they were treated as no more than subhuman beings. They were servants in every sense of the word, having no control whatsoever over their destiny.

What makes Peony's love affair unique, however, is that David's marriage has much bearing on the fate of the Ezra family. The Ezra household, being one of the last to hold on to its Jewish culture, faces extinction as a people through the acceptance by local Chinese. Madame Ezra, therefore, has always wanted to return to their promised land and to be a separate people. She tries desperately to preserve the family's Jewish traditions so as to keep its identity. Under her care, the customs and the ancient feasts at holiday times are religiously observed. When it comes to the marriage of David, her only son, she naturally insists on his marrying a Jewish girl, Leah, daughter of the only rabbi in the city. For she thinks that on David's marriage rests the duty of preserving the pure blood of God's chosen people against all odds in Chinese society.

But old beliefs and old customs cannot hold David's interest. Having a quarter Chinese blood in him, David is torn between his Jewish and Chinese heritages, confused as to which side he should belong. Besides, "The surge of young blood carried passions and a desire of action in today's world rather than allegiance to the past" ("Pearl S. Buck's *Peony*" 1948, 2). He is attracted to Kueilan, a Chinese girl, but he hesitates to disobey his mother's stern wish. We seem to have a love quadrangle here: Peony loves David, David loves Kueilan, while Leah also loves David and is the girl wanted by Madame Ezra to be David's future wife. What is at stake in this love affair is more than affections of those involved. It is the destiny of a people. It represents two strong, unconquerable social forces: the force of the Jews to remain a distinct people and the force of the well-meant warmth of the Chinese to obliterate such a distinction. Whatever Peony chooses to do is of significance, not only in her own fate, but also in the fate of the Jews.

Since any over-the-limit display of affection toward David would mean departure from him to a world where she "knew no one" and "had not a friend" (34), Peony realizes that she has to "live with it [her fate] and within it, yielding to it, accepting it, becoming part of it" (84), while at the same time valuing every opportunity she has to serve David.

What life offers Peony, however, is less than this: she might even lose the opportunity to serve David. Madame Ezra has arranged for Leah to come to the Ezra household so as to win over David's heart. Peony knows that Leah, who has been a playmate of hers, is "a woman strong enough to win a man entirely and hold him so" (42). As a result, Leah might not allow her to stay in the house. Here we see another aspect of a bondmaid's life: Although she may be loved and respected to some extent, she could be easily discarded once she was not wanted. She has none of the protections that other women, such as wives and mothers, have. She is no more than a lifeless object whose value is judged solely by her usefulness to the master's family.

If the young Peony does not yet know the essence of life for a bondmaid, Wang Ma does. Through her own experience, particularly the long dead pipe dreams she has had about her own master, Ezra, Wang Ma knows only too well what to expect from life for people like her and Peony. When Peony comes to her for consultation, she says: "Life is sad" (83). This seeming philosophical statement is a conclusion that a Chinese women servant has drawn from her own experience.

Tragedy does not end with Peony's inability to control her fate with David. Later, when a wicked yet powerful steward from the Imperial Court shows interest in her, Peony cannot refuse on grounds that she does not love him, because doing so will bring harm to David's business and even danger to the Ezra family. Therefore, she becomes a nun, the only alternative for her to escape the desire of the steward.

Although she cannot control her own fate, Peony knows how to make the best of her position, to utilize the limited means she has to achieve what she thinks she deserves—a characteristic found in all women characters dealt with in this study. The difference between Peony and other women, such as the mother in *The Mother*, O-lan in *The Good Earth*, and Madame Wu in *Pavilion of Women*, is that she seems to be more manipulative and her means more covert. This is due to the unique, unfavorable situation she finds herself in—as a single woman out on her own, she lacks the kind of protection, help, or support other women might have, thus having to rely solely on her own wit. She decides to arrange David's marriage and, in doing so, unconsciously arranges the end of a Jewish family.

Once having realized that she cannot be wedded to David, Peony, upon the advice of Wang Ma, decides to play a part in choosing a wife for David. Between Leah and Kueilan, Kueilan is obviously the better choice. First, Kueilan will not drive her out of the Ezra family. Second, she believes that David is attracted more to Kueilan than to Leah because David has once openly announced that he does not love Leah. If she cannot marry David, she wants David to be happy to marry the one he wants. Third, she believes that Leah, being a Jew herself, will only remind David of their past. Kueilan, on the other hand, will take him "away from the dark, sorrowful people to whom he had been born and bring him into the pleasant sunshine in which her people lived. He would forget death and learn to love life" (103).

She does not at all despise the Jewish people:

> She supposed that they revered their ancestors and preserved their traditions exactly as the Chinese did. But she grieved that so many of these traditions were sorrowful ones and because she loved David she wanted to persuade him that he would be happier if he forgot that he was a chosen one . . . for, she reasoned, since life itself is sad, our years so few and death so certain and swift, why not be happy in the short between? Convinced of sadness, she determined to rejoice in whatever bit of life came her way, and by her love she set the handsome young Jew on what she thought was the road to happiness. At least it led away from the old deep sorrows of his own people. (8)

These three reasons for helping David to marry Kueilan reveal several important characteristics of Peony. First, we see some good qualities of her: while securing her place in the family is one of the motivations, it is not the only one. In other words, she helps Kueilan not entirely out of selfishness, but to enable David to marry the one she thinks he loves. This falls little short of nobility. Second, her purpose of helping David out of his "sorrowful past," while perhaps also out of kindness, suggests arrogance: although she claims that she does not despise the Jewish people, she believes that the Chinese live in the "pleasant sunshine" and that marrying a Chinese woman is the "road to happiness."

Therefore, Peony immediately takes action to help Kueilan, or rather, David. She finishes the poem David has started to write for Kueilan and sends it to her. She then finds out that Kueilan is also attracted to David. Since Kueilan can barely read and write, she forges a poem for Kueilan to return to David. She then arranges for David to meet Kueilan in secret so the relationship between them can develop, for it was not easy for a man and a woman to meet freely then.

Regardless of how well she means, Peony never realizes that her actions have far-reaching implications for the Ezra family and the Jewish people in general. Because of her effort, the relationship between David and Kueilan develops further, which causes Leah's suicide, a tragedy for both the rabbi's family and the Ezras. More importantly, the marriage between David and Kueilan symbolizes an assimilation of the Jews into the Chinese, something that the Jewish people fear most.

It is here that we see a deep irony, an irony that Buck apparently did not intend: Good intentions of the Chinese have produced disastrous consequences for the Jews. This suggests a lack of understanding between the two peoples: The Chinese do not realize how important it is for the Jews to retain their identity. They try to melt the Jewish people in their warmth, believing that such melting is for their benefit. The Jews perhaps do not understand the Chinese either: Had the Ezra family found out what Peony has done, they would be very much angered, for Peony has intruded into their own life, making decisions for them, and taking their fate into her own hands. This is hardly the kind of mutual understanding Buck claims to promote. It is mutual misunderstanding and cultural conflict.

In terms of characterization, these actions make Peony stand out a little above the typical image of bondmaid—she is capable of reasoning, rather calculative, and courageous. She is willing and able to act on her own to manipulate the Ezra family, changing the life of a community of people. While this might appear imposing to the Western reader, it is arguably justifiable by her good intention: She believes that she is doing her best to help others. This is in line with the Chinese concept of warmth discussed at the outset of the chapter.

Putting things together, we find that Peony is capable of deep thought, intelligent, rather calculating, and full of self-sacrifice. For David's sake as well as for her own, she dares to run the risk of being driven out of the house when she arranges the meeting between David and Kueilan. She refuses to be David's concubine so that he can have peace with his own conscience. When the evil steward puts pressure on David to give her up, she would not risk bringing any harm to David's family by staying in their house. She sacrifices her own love and happiness by becoming a nun, providing David the opportunity to develop love with Kueilan. Even when she sees later that David has become in love with his wife, Peony hardly has any feeling of jealousy, although the pain lingers.

Putting aside her intelligence and ability to change the life of many and her courageous effort to take control of her own fate, we find that most of Peony's traits, actions, and the ups and downs in her life are somewhat predictable to those familiar with the Chinese culture. Her poor family background, her good behavior, the love and respect she gains from the family, her close relationship with the master and later her love for him, the agony she suffers because of the impossibility of marrying him, and most important of all, her oppression by society so that she has no way to control her own fate no matter how hard she tries, are common among bondmaids. In other words, Peony is more typical than individualized. On the typicality–individuality continuum, Peony as a character falls somewhere more toward the typicality end than the individuality end.

A less individualized character does not stand out as sharply as a more individualized character. This perhaps accounts for some reviewers' opinions that Buck "has been content to tell a tale without lavishing much care on developing her characters . . ." (Ross 1948, 17). However, what seems to be lost in the lack of individualization is more than made up by the author's ability to use "that little box of tricks that we associated exclusively with feminine fiction" (Voiles 1948, 18), and reviewers agree that Peony is a very lovable and vividly drawn character. The reader is led to go through every step of Peony's life crisis, to feel every change of her emotions, to struggle with her inner conflicts, to reason with her out of her frustrations, and, finally, to see her carry on, composed, living with whatever she has and making the best of it.

Moreover, Buck's characterization of Peony is closely related to the overall theme of the novel. *Peony* would strike the reader as a touching love story: at least one reviewer, in the *New Yorker* (1948), seems to think so. But it is much more than that. In her review, for example, Mary Ross (1948) tells the readership that *Peony* shows "how and why Chinese succeeded effortlessly in effecting what has frustrated most of the Western world—obliterating a distinction between Jews and themselves" (17). Catherine Brown (1948) says that what Buck deals with in *Peony* is "the place of the Jews during the mid-nineteenth century, of their attempt to stand alone, and of their final benevolent Chinese amalgamation" (23). This interpretation of *Peony*'s theme is also shared by other reviewers (Scoggin 1948; Forbes 1948).

To bring out the theme of promoting peaceful racial coexistence— although this racial coexistence means the extinction for the Jews— Buck perhaps needed a more stereotypical character, one that she could use to represent the Chinese people. Reexamining Peony in this light, we see that Peony seems to be a good representative for Buck's purpose.

First, what Peony does in relation to her relationship with David is representative of Chinese women. A good Chinese woman, even nowadays, would wish her lover to find his love if he does not love her and leaves him if she decides that her own presence would be a hindrance to her lover's life and happiness. She suffers a lot of pain and might be jealous, but seldom does she complain, for she knows that love should be reciprocal. In this regard, Buck invites the reader to draw a comparison between Peony and Leah, the Jewish girl, who loves David perhaps as deeply as Peony. When she learns that David's heart is not on her, she becomes furious and hurts David with a sword that has once slain their people. Realizing what she has done, she kills herself with that very sword.

Second, Peony represents a conscious effort on the part of the Chinese to help the Jews get away from their unfortunate past and move to what they think will be a happy future. Although this turns out to be more of a disservice than a help to the Jews, being diametrically the opposite of what the Jews want, this conscious effort has its roots in the high value the Chinese put on being warm to and ready to help those in need. Thus, Peony embodies the Chinese's acceptance of a different people—their sympathy and understanding, their sincere welcome, and their spontaneous, conscious readiness to render help when needed, although all these characteristics might come out of their arrogance.

Since Buck's theme is problematic and her views of the Chinese attitude toward other people inconsistent, how can we interpret the characterization of Peony? Upon closer examination, we find that Buck's problems do not seem to have much negative bearing on her characterization. First, although Buck lets Peony claim that she treats the Jews as equals, we can easily detect the Chinese arrogance through her actions. Therefore, the image of the Chinese, particularly their arrogance, is not distorted. Second, although the Jewish people disagree with Buck on the idea of racial assimilation, it is a historical fact that the Jews were assimilated into the Chinese civilization and the conscious effort to facilitate such assimilation on the part of the Chinese was undoubtedly one of the reasons why the Jews were melted. Buck does not create the illusion that the Jews welcomed the assimilation and that the results of Peony's manipulation were positive. In fact, she provides us with a detailed account of how the Jews, represented by Madame Ezra, try their best to maintain their identity and depicts Leah's death as an indirect consequence of Peony's actions. This, perhaps, does not suggest a lack of understanding of the Jewish people on Buck's part, but her agreement with the Chinese that assimilation is a better alternative for them.

In conclusion, Peony the bondmaid is lovely, wise, kind and faithful. Peony the character is more typical than individualized, but successfully crafted and vividly portrayed. The characterization of a rather typical protagonist fits in well with the theme of the novel, illustrating Buck the novelist's craftsmanship and helping Peony the novel enjoy a good reputation among its large readership despite its problematic theme.

5

Peasant Women

IN *THE GOOD EARTH* AND *THE MOTHER* THE CHARACTERS SHARE THEIR HARD STRUGGLE for a better life against unfavorable natural conditions and, to a lesser degree, against the exploitation by their landlords. The main characters—O-lan in *The Good Earth* and the anonymous mother in *Mother*—are typical of Chinese women in their positions and at the same time individuals with their respective unique characteristics. O-lan is more individualized than the mother, and that difference is well explained by the themes of the novels in which they appear. Both characters use their limited power to achieve happiness for themselves as well as for their families, although each does this in her own way.

The Good Earth

It is generally acknowledged that *The Good Earth*, Pearl S. Buck's second novel, published in 1931, is by far the best and the most memorable. It became one of the most famous best-sellers both in and outside of the United States. Translated into more than thirty languages, it reached almost the entire reading world. With its success, *The Good Earth* won Pearl Buck the Pulitzer Prize in 1932 and the Howells Medal in 1935 for the most distinguished work of American fiction in five years. It was also an important factor in her winning the Nobel Prize in 1938.

The Good Earth, often praised as a Chinese peasant epic, tells the life cycle of birth, marriage, and death in the family of a peasant, Wang Lung. The story opens on Wang Lung's wedding day. Wang Lung, who has lived with his father his whole life, is to take a woman into their house. Unable to afford the wedding cost, his father has chosen a slave girl, O-lan, from the great House of Hwang to be his wife.

91

O-lan's coming brings great changes to the family. By her thriftiness and hard work, their old house is transformed into a clean, comfortable, and vibrant dwelling. O-lan works hard with her husband in the fields. Heaven is kind enough to grant them good harvest for a couple of years, and Wang Lung buys a piece of land from the House of Hwang. Additionally, O-lan gives birth to two sons in two consecutive years.

However, with the arriving of the third child, a female, which is seen as a bad omen at the time (as discussed in chapter 2), comes a famine resulting from a drought. Like thousands of others, the family has to go south where food is more plentiful. In order to make the trip, O-lan kills their fourth child, a daughter, at its birth. In the south, O-lan and the two boys beg on the streets while Wang Lung pulls a ricksha. To them, city life is strange and miserable and the only comfort is that their land is still awaiting them back home. Then the revolution breaks out. When the wealthy people of the town flee, the desperate poor break into their houses and loot. Wang Lung and O-lan, swept into the crowd, find themselves in possession of enough money to take them home.

Once back on their land, they continue to work hard. With the jewels O-lan obtains in the looting, Wang Lung purchases more and more land from the House of Hwang. Two more children are born and their house becomes the most prosperous around. Once rich, Wang Lung no longer goes to work in his fields, but to the teahouse in town where he lusts after Lotus, a prostitute. He finds O-lan no longer desirable for a man of his position and brings Lotus home to be his concubine. There is no peace in the house ever after. O-lan dies of a stomach illness and his father dies soon afterwards. Wang Lung's sons, educated and married, think nothing of the land and desire to live in the city. So they move into and finally buy the House of Hwang where O-lan used to be a slave. Though living a life of plenty now, Wang Lung has no peace, for there is always quarrelling in the house. Near the end of his life, Wang Lung, with his third young slave wife, Pear Blossom, goes back to live in the old house so as to find peace on his land, which, ironically, his two elder sons are plotting to sell.

The Good Earth, upon its publication, caught the reader's attention immediately. About its realism, Florence Ayscough wrote (1931):

> I have lived for many years in such a country and among such people as Mrs. Buck describes, and as I read her pages I smell once more the sweet scent of bean flowers opening in the spring . . .; all as it was and is there in the Yangtze Valley. (676)

Similarly, Paul Hutchinson (1931) pointed out that there had never been a novel that "looked more deeply and understandingly into actual Chinese life" (683). The novel's greatest effect, however, is that it humanizes the Chinese people for the American public. The readers feel a kinship toward Buck's characters, who engage their sympathies and with whom they could easily identify. Thus Carl Van Doren, in *The American Novel* (1940), commented that "*The Good Earth* for the first time made the Chinese seem as familiar as neighbors" (353). The writer of a review in *New Statesman and Nation* (1931) said:

> I can recall no novel that frees the ordinary, flesh and blood, everyday Chineseman so satisfyingly from those screens and veils and mirrors of artistic and poetic convention which nearly always make him, to the Western reader's eye, a flat and unsubstantial figure of a pale-colored ballet. (430)

Although Wang Lung is the main character, around whom the events in the novel revolve, O-lan seems able to gain more sympathy from the readers. A plain-looking, inarticulate, submissive, and enduring woman, O-lan plays a critical role in the ups and downs of Wang Lung and his family. Like the humble and wordless good earth, O-lan is rich in resources and silently produces and keeps life going. More than the good earth, O-lan is an intelligent, courageous, and capable woman, who makes the right decision at the right time for the family and keeps it going in health toward happiness.

In what follows, it will be shown that O-lan is a very individualized character while at the same time representative of the Chinese peasant women of her times. Like all other women, she is made aware of where her place is both in society and at home. She has also learned the principles of the Three Obediences and Four Virtues that society requires from a woman. However, it is important to see that, under such unfavorable situations, she is able to use her limited power to steer the fate of the family toward prosperity.

The first thing we notice of O-lan is her plain looks. Before we meet her for the first time, we already know from Wang Lung's father that she is not supposed to be a pretty woman, whom a poor house like theirs does not need. At first glance, she appears to be "a square, rather tall figure," with "neat and smooth" hair, and "clothed in clean blue cotton coat and trousers." And "He [Wang Lung] saw with an instant's disappointment that her feet were not bound" (20). Looking more closely, Wang Lung finds out that:

> She had a square, honest face, a short, broad nose with large black nostrils, and her mouth was wide as a gash in her face. Her eyes were small and of a dull black in color, and were filled with some sadness that was not clearly expressed. It was a face that seemed habitually silent and unspeaking, as though it could not speak if it would . . . there was not beauty of any kind in her face—a brown, common, patient face. (22)

The only thing Wang Lung can comfort himself with is that she has no pockmarks on her dark skin and her lips are not split.

As for O-lan's personality, Buck lets us view her first through the eyes of the Old Mistress of the House of Hwang. According to the Old Mistress, O-lan is a "good slave, although somewhat slow and stupid," "does well what she is told to do and she has a good temper" (21). Next, Buck has Wang Lung, who is naturally eager and curious to find out what his bride is really like, watch her closely for the next few months after their marriage.

To Wang Lung, O-lan seems to be dull and slow. For instance, when Wang Lung wants to know if there is a side gate on their way out of the House of Hwang, "she nodded after a little thought, as though she did not understand too quickly what he said" (23). All the way out of the house, where she has been a slave for ten years, her face is expressionless, and her eyes "dumb" when she looks at him. Above all, the reader is constantly struck by O-lan's silence. "She never talked . . . except for the brief necessities of life" (32). She does everything in her submissive ways, a virtue she has been forced to adopt. When Wang Lung shows her the box and the basket to take home, she places the heavy box on her shoulder without a word. When Wang Lung changes his mind and commands her to take the basket instead, she simply obeys, "still speechless." Once a wife, she does her daily chores without a word; she works with Wang Lung in the fields quietly. Even in childbirth, she is silent. She appears so inarticulate that one wonders if she is capable of thinking. Wang Lung could make nothing of her. So he contents himself with the thought that she is, after all, only a woman.

However, this seemingly ordinary peasant wife surprises the reader more and more as the story goes on. As we observe more of her, especially after she is out of the House of Hwang, we find that the Old Mistress is not altogether right about her. Even Wang Lung has quite a few surprises from O-lan's intelligence and ability. He admits to himself that "she was a woman such as not commonly found" (40).

We find, as the story reveals little by little, that O-lan is not only hardworking, dutiful, enduring, but also intelligent, competent, and has a practical mind to get things done toward good. Silent or inarticulate though she may be, she carries with her a quiet dignity that catches the reader's heart.

Evidence of O-lan's good qualities is bountiful throughout the novel. Her image as a hardworking, dutiful, and enduring woman who always serves as a provider is set from the very first day of the wedding. According to Chinese custom, even a girl from a poor family gets to wear red, has the day off from daily chores, and is waited upon on her wedding day. O-lan, however, never gets to enjoy what a wife is normally entitled to. She has no wedding clothes and no formal wedding ceremony. Out of the House of Hwang, on their way toward the small earthen house of his ancestors, they stop to burn incense before the gods in the wayside temple to the earth, which is supposedly the moment of their marriage. She has to start working hard to fulfill her duty as a wife as soon as she steps into Wang Lung's house. The only celebration they have is the wedding "feast," but O-lan is the one who prepares it and stays in the kitchen, working the entire time until all the guests are gone. Through the wedding feast, O-lan not only proves her own capability but also brings Wang Lung the pride he has never had among his folks, for with what little meat she has, she has "skillfully brought forth all the force of the meat itself, so that Wang Lung himself had never tasted such dishes upon the tables of his friends" (27).

As the wedding feast symbolizes, O-lan, in the days to come, takes what little life has to offer her and makes the best of it. Rather than just doing well what she is told to do, as the Old Mistress says about her, she does the daily chores "without a word and without being commanded to do them" (32). Every day, she is the first one to arise at dawn to light the stove and the last one to go to bed at midnight after making sure every household matter has been well taken care of. Furthermore, she goes to work with Wang Lung in the fields. Thus, she actually works much harder than Wang Lung, for she has the extra housework to do, meals to prepare, and the ox to be fed after a whole tiresome day's work in the fields. She never stops working, even when she is heavy with child. Except for the firstborn, O-lan will stop working in the fields only when she had to go back to deliver. Right afterward, she would come back to work at Wang Lung's side as if she had done nothing extraordinary. Even for the first childbirth, she surprises Wang Lung by stopping in her labor to prepare food for him and his father. When her family becomes rich, she refuses to use a slave and insists on doing everything by herself until too sick to work anymore.

It is interesting to note that O-lan's diligence is both typical of Chinese peasant women and unique to herself. The Chinese people are noted for their willingness to work hard, and Chinese women are even more capable of doing so simply because they have more responsibilities than men. However, O-lan's diligence seems to exceed that of peasant women in general. For example, we can safely say that very few women are able to prepare food for their family during childbirth labor. This interdependence of typicality and individualization well illustrates Buck's skill in characterization: individualization, although seemingly the opposite to typicality, grows out of typicality rather than running counter to it.

O-lan never complains, seldom asks anything for herself for all the work she has done, and endures quietly any hardship that comes her way, both physically and emotionally. For her endurance, the reader can hardly forget the vivid scenes of her child delivering. One critic, Barbara LeBar (1988), rightly points out that O-lan makes mockery of modern "natural" childbirth. O-lan "simply has a child. And she bears it alone—without a doctor, without a midwife, without even her husband" (265), and, I would like to add, without a scream. Furthermore, she goes back to work beside her husband without a word right after she gives birth to their second son, thinking not about herself but that the rice has to be gathered into sheaves before the rain.

During the year of famine, the entire family starves, but O-lan is the one who suffers most. Here is what Wang Lung sees after O-lan kills the infant girl to avoid another mouth to feed:

> Her eyes were closed and the color of her flesh was the color of ashes and her bones stuck under the skin—a poor silent face that lay there, having endured to the utmost, and there was nothing he [Wang Lung] could say. After all, during these months he had only his own body to drag about. But this woman had endured what agony of starvation with the starved creature gnawing at her from within, desperate for its own life! (86)

Apart from physical hardships, O-lan endures much emotional pain. When Wang Lung gets tired of O-lan and becomes infatuated with Lotus, he reproaches her for not dressing properly and having feet too big to be fit for a landowner's wife. O-lan takes the reproach humbly and hides her feet under the bench. At Wang Lung's anger, she only says in a whisper: "My mother did not bind them, since I was sold so young. But the little girl's feet I will bind" (176).

The most unbearable thing that O-lan confronts is the time when Wang Lung forces her to give up the two pearls, which she wants to keep not for her own sake, but as a future wedding gift for her younger daughter. When Wang Lung laughs at the sight of the pearls O-lan puts in his hands,

> O-lan returned to the beating of his clothes and when tears dropped slowly and heavily from her eyes she did not put up her hand to wipe them away; only she beat the more steadily with her wooden stick upon the clothes spread over the stones. (194)

When Wang Lung takes Lotus into the house, O-lan goes to work in the fields and comes back silently, saying nothing to anyone, and goes into the kitchen to do her duty as she always does. At night, she sleeps alone by herself, burying her sorrow all in her heart.

One wonders how O-lan could endure so much in silence. Is she really dull and not capable of thinking? Wang Lung cannot make anything of her, thus giving up his attempt to understand her. However, the discerning reader would find that O-lan is anything but dull.

O-lan's silent endurance of hardship and pain has its roots in the mistreatment women of her times received from society. As indicated in chapter 2, Chinese society offered women so little that they had learned to expect little from life. Even to gain that little, they had to make much effort and to endure the kind of suffering that their male counterparts did not. This is especially true for a woman like O-lan, who comes from the bottom of society as a slave girl. Having been freed from slavery and becoming a landowner's wife is already more than she could expect; any hardship in this capacity would seem nothing compared with what she has had to endure as a slave.

O-lan's silence can also be explained by her miserable past experiences. Having been sold at the age of ten to the House of Hwang in times of famine, O-lan has been severely oppressed and mistreated for ten years. From her habitual slavegirl gesture of raising her arms as if to defend herself from a blow, and her brief unconscious words in her last hours, we gather that she has been forced to accept the fact that she is ugly and therefore not to be loved. Even among the slaves, she is at the bottom, not even allowed to appear before the great lord of the house. She has been beaten for the smallest mistake she makes and anyone can scold her for no fault of her own. There is no place for her to speak. Besides, women were viewed as inferior and supposed to be submissive to men. So, once married to Wang Lung, she tries to do all in her silent obedience. Her silence is therefore one of her trademarks, indicating her personality, her background, and her effort to make her behavior acceptable.

Despite the oppression, O-lan, like other women, "has her joys and sorrows and experiences a full range of human emotions" (Li 1989, 99). In her
silence we see her pride, desire, stubbornness, and temper. She is proud of
the fact that she is doing well as Wang Lung's wife, for there is "not one
slave with a new coat like mine" in the House of Hwang; she is proud of
her first son because "there was not even a child among the concubines of
the Old Master himself to compare to him in beauty and in dress" (54). She
is also proud of having been a mother, who has produced so many sons for
the family. Such pride, as Doyle (1980) comments, "is particularly touching because O-lan wants and expects so little from life" (36).

O-lan has a love for beauty. When she hands all the jewels to Wang
Lung, she asks to keep two smooth white pearls for herself. At this,

> Wang Lung, without comprehending it, looked for an instant into the heart
> of this dull and faithful creature, who had labored all her life at some task at
> which she won no reward and who in the great house had seen others wear-
> ing jewels which she never even felt in her hand once. (153)

To his puzzled eyes, O-lan only says: "I could hold them in my hand sometimes" (153). Later, when Wang Lung cruelly takes them from her to give
to Lotus, O-lan said nothing, but her tears, which have been seldom shed,
suggest that she is heartbroken.

The quiet O-lan also possesses self-dignity. For instance, while she tol-
erates Lotus for Wang Lung's sake, she refuses to serve or speak to Cuckoo,
who, when a superior in the House of Hwang, was cruel and picky. She
protests to Wang Lung, which she seldom does, against the presence of
Cuckoo in her house and shows her disdain by ignoring Cuckoo's existence. She says, "with a sullenness deeper than ever upon her face, 'I am not
slave of slaves in this house at least'" (213).

O-lan is in fact very intelligent, thoughtful, and much more practical
than Wang Lung—qualities that seem to have been lost in her silence. She
is like a pond of still water that runs deep. Buck only occasionally offers
her reader the opportunity to glance at her depth. For instance, before she
and her husband return to visit the House of Hwang with their firstborn, O-
lan astonishes Wang Lung with her careful planning. He has not expected
her, with the way she has gone about her work, to have thought about their
unborn child and what she will do when she returns to the house where she
used to be a slave. But he finds the child fully clothed and the mother in a
new coat also (37). It turns out that, although she says nothing while work-

ing by his side in the fields, she has been making plans for the event by herself all along.

O-lan's intelligence is shown in many cases—not only in terms of the way she sees things, but also in terms of how she expresses her own opinion and gets things done while still seeming to remain obedient and submissive. When Wang Lung first thinks of buying land from Hwang, she responds with much shrewdness. Though, at first, she does not think that buying land from Huang is a good idea, she does not immediately state her opinion against Wang Lung. Instead, she makes it clear that she supports his idea of buying land, for she thinks it better than putting money into a mud wall. Meanwhile, she shows more consideration for the practicality of buying land from Hwang, pointing out that the land is too far away and they would have to walk the whole morning to reach it. Seeing that Wang Lung's mind is set on buying it, however, she submits to his decision, again thinking about it in more practical terms: "rice land is good, and it is near the moat and we can get water every year" (56).

During the famine, she helps Wang Lung to resist his uncle and two city slickers who have been pressing him to sell their land. She sees farsightedly that if they sold the land then, they would have nothing to feed themselves when they return from the south. She will sell the furniture since they have to move, but she will not sell the hoes and plows, which they will need to work on the land. In the city, it is O-lan who is shrewd enough to know what kind of mats are the best buy and clever enough to shape them into a comparatively comfortable hut, with a rounded roof and a matted floor, as a family shelter.

O-lan is also more practical than Wang Lung in many other ways. Wang Lung cannot bear to kill the ox and eat the meat, while O-lan sees an ox as an ox, which should be sacrificed to save human lives. Similarly, when their second son brings home some meat, Wang Lung throws it away because it is stolen. O-lan simply picks up the meat, washes the dirt off and puts it back into the boiling pot, for "Meat is meat," as she says quietly, and it is the time of famine.

However, in doing all this, O-lan never lets herself appear more intelligent than Wang Lung, never complains or criticizes Wang Lung for his improper behavior, and almost never openly speaks a word against him. When Wang Lung is incapable of carrying out a certain task, she takes things over in her own hands only as if simply to complete what Wang Lung has left unfinished. She knows that she ought to appear subordinate to her husband.

Though O-lan does not speak, she sees everything clearly. It is she who senses the incestuous relationship between their eldest son and Lotus and suggests sending him away to the south to avoid a family scandal. She also discerns that Wang Lung is more and more like the lords in the great house and that what has happened in the House of Hwang would happen in their family. However, she is now helpless, as Wang Lung has forsaken her. She knows that Wang Lung does not love her, a fact that Wang Lung later learns from his daughter. Wang Lung feels sad "because with all her dimness O-lan had seen the truth in him" (260).

When O-lan chooses to speak, she does it logically and forcefully. Here is what she says to the villagers who come to loot their house:

> It is not yet time to take our table and the benches and the bed from our house. You have all our food. But out of your own houses you have not sold yet your table and your benches. Leave us ours. We are even. We have not a bean or a grain of corn more than you—no, you have more than we, now, for you have all of ours. Heaven will strike you if you take more. Now, we will go out together and hunt for grass to eat and bark from the trees, you for your children, and we for our three children, and for this fourth who is to be born in such times. (78)

When she marries Wang Lung, O-lan knows what is expected of her and, compared to being a slave, her social status is instantly elevated. Therefore, she does not mind the hard work as a wife and takes a submissive position to her husband. Besides, she cares very much for Wang Lung, to whom she gives all her devotion and for whose happiness she will do anything. The reason for her silence is not that she does not know how to speak, but because she has deliberately chosen not to speak and has long formed such a habit. Though we know that she is often more shrewd than Wang Lung, she never shows it off and is always supportive and submissive to Wang Lung's will. Only when compelled by crises, when Wang Lung is too weak-minded to deal with the situation, does she come forward. When this happens, she is still supportive to her husband, never making him feel embarrassed. She does what has to be done or says what has to be said when needed.

Putting all these good qualities—endurance, silence, intelligence, resourcefulness, and practicality—together, we see in O-lan a very individualized character. Her individuality, it should be noted, is believable as well, because it embodies the typical characteristics of the Chinese peasant women in her times and reflects the actual social conditions under which she lives.

O-lan manages not only to achieve some measure of happiness and autonomy for herself, but also brings love, warmth, and comfort into Wang Lung's house and steers Wang Lung's life toward success, wealth, and happiness. Before O-lan's coming to the house, Wang Lung has to take care of the house and his old father besides working daily in the fields. Life is miserable for him. With O-lan's coming, his life turns dramatically from the first day of his wedding, when O-lan takes all the household chores over to herself. Wang Lung begins to enjoy "this luxury of living" (28) he has never had before. Now, he can afford to lie "in his bed warm and satisfied," "tasting and savoring in his mind and flesh his luxury of idleness" "while in the kitchen the woman fed the fire and boiled the water" (29). Even hard work in the fields becomes a luxury, because when it is done he can go back to his house, which O-lan has made clean and comfortable, and where food is always ready and delicious for his appetite.

With O-lan's diligence, thriftiness, and skillful management, the family's livelihood is much improved. Before marrying O-lan, no matter how hard Wang Lung worked, they were poor. Now they are able to save money on fuel and fertilizer, for O-lan gathers them herself. With O-lan working with him in the fields, he is even able to have some extra money at the harvest time to buy a piece of land. More importantly, O-lan has produced children, especially sons, one after another, rendering the house full of life.

Apart from the physical changes O-lan has brought to Wang Lung's life, she gives Wang Lung pride, happiness, and confidence. Just look how proud Wang Lung is at the wedding feast, how delighted when their first son is born, and how happy when he gives the red eggs to his friends and the villagers to celebrate the "big happiness." "Wang Lung felt his heart fit to burst with pride. There was no other woman in the village able to do what his had done, to make cakes such as only the rich ate at the feast" (50). When they go to the House of Hwang, with his whole family dressed in new clothes O-lan has made and the cakes O-lan has prepared, Wang Lung, for the first time in his life, holds his head high with self-esteem.

These are enough to illustrate O-lan's importance in Wang Lung's life. But O-lan does more. If any ordinary wife can accomplish what O-lan has done to make the life of the family better, O-lan is quite extraordinary for her crucial actions at critical times to steer her husband's and the family's fate.

The first extraordinary act of O-lan is the killing of the ox in the time of famine. It is not that O-lan has a harder heart, but that she knows that, with nothing else to eat, the ox must be killed for the family to survive. Besides, as she sees it: "Eat, for there will be another one day and far better than this one" (76). The meat of the ox saves the family from starving to death.

Another critical moment is when the villagers, driven by hunger and desperation, come to loot Wang Lung's house. It is O-lan who, with her pregnant belly, brings them back to their senses. Later, by selling these bits of furniture O-lan has saved, they are able to make the trip to the south.

When Wang Lung, in a moment of weakness, is about to agree to sell their land for a little money to feed the family, O-lan comes forward to prevent it. When she is talking, "There was some calmness in her voice which carried more strength than Wang Lung's anger" (92). Afterward, O-lan helps Wang Lung to make up his mind to go south.

The most shocking thing O-lan does, especially to the Western eye, may be the killing of her second infant girl at its birth. However, her "reasons for so acting," as Ms. LeBar says (1988), "are as compelling as any in fact or fiction" (265). Firstly, they could not afford to feed another mouth when the whole family is already starved. Secondly, in her condition, she herself cannot possibly feed the new baby, who, therefore, cannot survive for long anyway. Thirdly, O-lan does it so that they can have less worry and difficulty to make the trip to the south, which, as it later turns out, will save the life of the whole family. Weighing the pros and cons, knowing Wang Lung does not want this girl at such a time, O-lan makes the decision to do the unimaginable and takes the guilt all to herself. LeBar thinks that O-lan "terminated an unwanted pregnancy in a way not too much different from the way it is done in modern times at local abortion clinics" (265). To explain this seemingly cruel action, Pearl Buck says, in My Several Worlds (1954):

> It was inevitable that the very reality of their lives made them sometimes cruel. A farm woman could strangle her own newborn girl baby if she were desperate enough at the thought of another mouth added to the family, but she wept while she did it and the weeping was raw sorrow, not simply at what she did, but far deeper, over the necessity she felt to do it. (146)

Wang Lung's rise to wealth owes much to O-lan, particularly to the jewelry O-lan discovers in a rich man's house during a looting. Taking the jewelry may suggest dishonesty on O-lan's part, but the situation O-lan is placed in seems to justify her act. First, this is something O-lan would not normally do if she were not swept into the mass looting. Second, having been a slave in a rich man's house before, she knows how extravagantly the rich live. When her family faces starvation, it is only human for her to take whatever comes her way. Besides, as Li Bo noted (1989),

> It was not an uncommon thing in China during the 1920s and 1930s for the poor people to break into rich people's houses and seize their properties because they regarded the rich as their oppressors and exploiters. O-lan never felt guilty about her robbery because it was not considered a bad thing in her time. (101)

The jewels O-lan gets enables Wang Lung to buy more and more land and finally takes Wang Lung to the position he has never dreamed of reaching. Wang Lung himself knows in his heart that all the riches he has gotten would have been impossible if O-lan had not found the jewels and had not given them to him when he commanded her.

What is more important, O-lan is the central good force of the family, serving as a cohesive tie to hold the family together. With O-lan as the wife and mother, there is plenty of love, warmth, comfort, and a healthy atmosphere in the house, which, as Doan (1965) points out, "are essential for family happiness" (76). The old father becomes healthy and contented; the children are well cared for, among whom the retarded daughter receives special attention; Wang Lung himself is satisfied and happy, at least for the first several years.

From this, we see that it is O-lan who sees the family through all the crises; it is O-lan who gets done what has to be done; it is O-lan who holds the family together; and it is O-lan on whom Wang Lung's wealth and fate rest. No wonder that, to Buck, O-lan, with her almost inexhaustible resource of life, symbolizes the good earth which has borne and sustained the life of the Chinese peasants for more than two thousand years:

> The woman [O-lan] and the child were as brown as the soil and they sat there like figures made of earth. . . . But out of the woman's great brown breast the milk gushed forth for the child . . . it flowed like a fountain . . . life enough for many children, and she let it flow out carelessly, conscious of her abundance. (44)

The crucial role O-lan plays in the family is significant in many ways. First, it adds much individuality to O-lan as a complex, dynamic character, making her unique and memorable. Second, it reflects Buck's feminist point of view. *The Good Earth* is considered an epic, telling the ups and downs

of Wang Lung, but it is O-lan who is the driving force for his rise to prosperity and higher social status.

As if the events discussed thus far are not enough to suggest O-lan's
importance, Buck sets up a contrast in Wang Lung's family between the
time when he works with O-lan and the time when he turns away from her.
During the former time, Wang Lung's family survives crisis one after another and gradually obtains prosperity. However, as soon as Wang Lung
turns away from O-lan, love, warmth, and peace vanish from the house and
lust, quarrelling, and sickness set in. Wang Lung's morality deteriorates
greatly once he turns from O-lan to Lotus. He thinks himself entitled to
frequenting the teahouse in town and having concubines, giving no consideration to O-lan's feelings. He becomes a brute, pouring all his anger upon
O-lan because she is too common, too ugly to suit his new status.

Yet Lotus, whom Wang Lung feels he needs now as a rich man and later
takes home to be his second wife, is nothing more than a sexual object for
Wang Lung, a toy for him to play with. Once Wang Lung becomes infatuated with Lotus, he neglects O-lan entirely. He never notices that O-lan's
health has greatly deteriorated and "he had not thought why she had been
willing at last to stay in the house and why she moved slowly and more
slowly about" (262). O-lan finally dies of a stomach illness, due to much
hardship, fatigue, and a long time of neglect of her disease.

Without O-lan, the house falls apart: "for the first time Wang Lung and
his children knew what she had been in the house, and how she made comfort for them all and they had not known it" (265). No one seems to know
how to light the stove and how to cook and no one bothers to clean the
house. The retarded girl is once left outside in the cold the whole night and
almost dies from the illness she gets as a result. The old father is neglected
and dies soon after O-lan's death. There are plenty of women in the house,
but Wang Lung knows in his heart that there will never be the kind of love and
care O-lan once gave him and his children. The house is divided and declining.

As a representative of the old-fashioned Chinese country women, a Confucian model of a caring mother and a faithful wife, O-lan's qualities are
more appreciated when compared to other, minor characters in the novel: Wang
Laung's concubines Lotus and Pear Blossom, and Cuckoo, Lotus's slave.

Lotus is everything O-lan is not. She entices Wang Lung because she
loves his money. It is therefore no surprise that she contributes nothing to
the family but jealousy and turmoil. While O-lan is the central force that
unites the family, Lotus is a bad disease, infecting and weakening it. Every
time Wang Lung is with Lotus, he comes home ill-tempered toward every-

one. With her, Wang Lung does not only part from O-lan, but is also shunned by his children. To make it worse, Lotus develops an incestuous relationship with Wang Lung's eldest son, bringing shame and pain to the family.

Pear Blossom, a young girl whom Wang Lung takes as a third wife in his old age, shares some similarity with O-lan. She remains faithful to Wang Lung and takes care of the retarded daughter for O-lan until the end of her days. However, she lacks the kind of courage and ability we have seen in O-lan.

Cuckoo, a slave, cannot compare to O-lan, a former slave herself. She is a snob, bullying fellow slave girls below her position but fawning on her superiors and the rich, from whom she thinks she can benefit. When her master is rich, she tries to entice him. Once his family's wealth collapses, she betrays him. She uses the money she has taken from the old master to run a teahouse, but when she sees less work and more comfort and security to be gained in going into Wang Lung's house with Lotus, she chooses to be a slave again. Her behavior is even despised by O-lan, who, as we have seen, seldom thinks ill of others: "You may have lived in the courts of the Old Lord, and you were accounted beautiful, but I have been a man's wife and I have borne him sons, and you are still a slave" (269).

It is also interesting to compare O-lan with Madame Wu, in *Pavilion of Women*. At first sight, we see primarily differences. O-lan is quiet and inarticulate; Madame Wu is eloquent. O-lan does not come forward unless in some crisis that Wang Lung cannot handle; Madame Wu is always in the forefront of every family affair. O-lan does not have much control over the family decisions; Madame Wu is the maker of all decisions in the House of Wu. They even differ in appearance: While O-lan is plain-looking, Madame Wu is beautiful.

All these differences are, however, only superficial. They have many commonalities between them. They are both intelligent, courageous, hardworking, capable, and dignified; they both play crucial roles in the fate of their respective families.

How can we explain these differences on the one hand and similarities on the other, then? Such an explanation, in fact, is not hard to obtain. It can be sought in the origins of the two characters and the socioeconomic conditions they find themselves in. In terms of origin, O-lan's is humble whereas Madame Wu's is not. Having been a slave makes O-lan short of words and submissive. Being born and bred in a family of wealth provides Madame Wu the opportunity to be educated, thus becoming eloquent and dominant. In terms of socioeconomic conditions, O-lan is married into a poor peasant family, which means that her life will be characterized by hardship and submissiveness to her husband, whereas Madame Wu is wedded to a wealthy husband with a big family, which means that she will have the responsibility to oversee all affairs of the house, providing her with a stage to display all her intelligence and ability.

However, these differences do not necessarily prevent them from sharing positive qualities, qualities that can only be found in their very being. In other words, Buck may have offered the two characters different stages to perform and allowed them to act in different ways toward similar events in their respective lives, but she has bestowed on them the same nobility and admirability, hence the same credibility as literary characters.

O-lan possesses better qualities than her husband. O-lan, like many of Buck's Chinese women characters, is shown to have "more integrity, more steadfastness, more endurance in the crises and affairs of life" (Buck 1931, 905), while Wang Lung displays weakness in such situations. As he changes from a poor peasant to a wealthy landlord, he completely loses his integrity. He no longer works hard, and instead forsakes the land, takes concubines, betrays his wife, and lives an idle and corrupted life. In times of difficulty, he is happy and grateful to have O-lan as his wife. When he rises to prosperity, he deplores her ugliness and thinks that O-lan no longer fits his position.

Portraying Wang Lung as such does not only reveal Buck's conviction that Chinese women are better than men, but also that men's corruption has been caused, in part at least, by society. Buck tells us, through the narration, that Wang Lung is only doing what other men of wealth and leisure are supposed to do. Therefore, O-lan is, as Charles W. Hayford (1992) points out, "betrayed (but not broken) as much by her husband's weak character as by social attitudes" (12).

Through O-lan, Buck seems to suggest that, although oppressed, Chinese women, even the peasant women, have the same fine qualities as women elsewhere in the world. They have strength, courage, and insight as well as a practical mind to steer the fate and future of a family and to struggle for dignity and happiness.

The Mother

When published in 1934, *The Mother* drew a great number of reviews. Such reviewers as G. R. B. Richards, Mark Van Doren, Herschel Brickell, and Isadore Schneider seemed to agree that the central character, the mother, is universal in nature, embodying mothers of all races. Despite this consensus, the novel evoked great controversy among its critics. Its simplicity in style, for instance, was believed to be a strength by some, such as J. Donald Adams, Mark Van Doren, Mary Ross, and Fanny Butcher, and boring and monotonous by others, such as Geoffrey Stone and Paul Doyle.

The second controversy, which is more relevant to the present study, centers on whether or not the mother as a character is individualized. After commenting on the universality of the mother, for example, Mark Van Doren writes (1934):

> But it is worthy of note that she [Buck] has not been able to avoid individualizing her people. The mother, the father, each one of the children, the cousin, the landlord's agent who seduces the mother, the village gossip—not one of these but has his uniqueness and picturesque clarity. At the same time that the book reminds us of the similarity which human beings bear to one another it reminds us of the fact that no two of them are identical. (78)

On the other hand, there are those who think that the mother is a faceless character. Garnett writes:

> The mother . . . is not an individual; she is Any Mother from among all of China's teeming millions. Thus she has no personal characteristics; she has not even a name. She is just an abstract figure of maternity: The Mother. (120)

Doyle (1980) agrees with this as well when he says that "The basic fault with *The Mother* is that she becomes too much a type and too little a realized individual" (65).

The following analysis, however, will exhibit that the mother possesses both typicality and individuality. She is typical enough to embody characteristics of all mothers and individualized enough to be unique and memorable. Compared to O-lan, however, she is less individualized, which is called for by Buck's intention to create a universal mother. We will also see that the mother, as other major women characters in Buck's novels, uses whatever little power and recourse she has to achieve what she thinks she deserves, even when it means a little calculation and a little deception.

Reading *The Mother*, one cannot help but wonder at its seemingly plotless structure. The mother works hard in the fields with her husband and at home with household chores. But the husband is not satisfied with the ordinary peasant life and therefore leaves the mother to go to a far-off town for his own pleasure. The mother is left with the full responsibility for the family, which includes an old grandmother and three young children, one of whom, a girl, is partially blind.

Besides having to provide for the family, the mother faces the humiliation that she has been abandoned by her man. Therefore, she forges letters from her husband, saying that he has found a good job in that town and is able to send some money back home. During this time, the landlord's agent, who comes to the village annually to collect grain for the landlord, seduces the mother. They have only one sexual encounter but the mother becomes pregnant and the agent deserts her. She purchases some herbal medicine to abort the child and her health deteriorates as a result.

Later she finds her oldest son a wife and, because the young couple do not think it their responsibility to provide for the blind sister, the mother marries her to a poor family in another village over the hill. The blind girl dies sometime later, possibly as a result of mistreatment. Then the youngest son, who has become a Communist, is executed by the government. The mother is ready to die of grief, but her fire of life rekindles when she sees her newly born grandson, whose arrival she has been awaiting for eight years.

Thus is the life story of the mother. The plot is the least dramatic and complicated among all Buck's novels. However, Buck creates a universal image of mother against this simple backdrop with considerable success, demonstrating her artistry and literary skills.

The reader first sees in the mother her love of hard work. Before her husband leaves the family, her day begins thus:

> In the morning the mother woke and rose before dawn, and while the others still slept she opened the door and let out the fowls and the pig and led the water buffalo into the dooryard, and she swept up what filth they had dropped in the night and put it upon the pile at a corner of the dooryard. While the others still lay she went into the kitchen and lit the fire and made water hot for the man and for the old woman to drink when they woke, and some she poured into a wooden basin to cool a little, so that she might wash the girl's face. (25)

This narration may strike some as tedious. But this tediousness of the narration reflects the tediousness of the life of the mother: she has to do all these things every morning, and the morning chores are only a small part of her day. After setting everything in order, she will go to the fields with her man, working no less than him, in cold winter days and hot summer days alike. During lunch time, the man takes a break, but the mother cooks for the family. When they come back home at dusk, the man's job is done, but the mother still has to cook dinner, feeding everyone in the house.

The mother never complains about hard work. To her, hard work is part of her life and life in general. In those tedious, physically exhausting routines of her day she sees things that others do not:

> But she never felt them dull and she was well content with the round of the days. If any had asked her she would have made those bright black eyes of hers wide and said, "But the land changes from seedtime to harvest and there is the reaping of the harvest from our own land and the paying of the grain to the landlord from that land we rent, and there are the holidays of the festivals and of the new year, yes and even the children change and grow and I am busy bearing more, and to me there is naught but change, and change enough to make me work from dawn to dark, I swear." (28)

The mother is certainly an ordinary woman from a poor Chinese family. But she sees the essence of life, that change is embedded in the sameness of everyday life, that the extraordinary comes from the ordinary, and that it is the dull routines of everyday activities that keep life going forever. Therefore, she enjoys everything she does and, however tired she is by the end of the day, "she rose to every day with zest" (29).

After her husband leaves, the responsibility to provide for the family falls completely on the mother's shoulders. Her daily work is doubled, and there are some tasks that are simply too heavy for a woman to handle. She therefore seeks out help from her cousin with these tasks and carries on with the rest, providing her family with a decent living.

From all this, we see that the mother as a character is both universal and individualized. She is universal because she represents mothers of the world in her willingness to work and to sacrifice and in her endurance of hardships. She is individualized because she sees the essence of life.

Relating to this is the mother's second outstanding characteristic, that she, like O-lan, loves life itself despite the fact that life has offered her very little. She takes life the way it is and never loses her hope in it. "she was not one to think into the meanings of what passed before her, but only taking all that came for what it was" (209). She believes that "Life came and went at the appointed hour, and against such appointment there was no avail" (31). When her husband deserts her, she deals with it with tact, dignity, and the help of some deception (which will be discussed later) and lets life go on. After finding out that the landlord's agent is no longer interested in her, she wipes her tears, holds "her head high and free against the misty air" (177), then goes on with her motherly duties. When her blind daughter dies, she cries her heart out, and suffers the bereavement for months. However, she shakes off the pain herself by thinking that "'Aye, perhaps even what they say is true, perhaps it is better that my maid is dead. There are so many things worse than death.' And she held fast to this one thought" (261). At the end of the novel, she weeps for hours at the death of her youngest son, but, upon learning that a grandson has just been born, she runs to the room, "forgetting all the roomful she cried aloud, laughing as she cried, her eyes all swelled with her past weeping, 'See, cousin! I doubt I was so full of sin as once I thought I was, cousin—you see my grandson!'" (302).

One should remember that "destiny . . . rather than the landlord class is . . . the enemy in the Mother's futile struggle" (Schneider 1934, 136). The betrayal of the husband, the loss of the daughter by the mistreatment, possibly the murder of her family, and the loss of the youngest son, who is executed as a Communist, are all the product of China at that time, a China that was characterized by material poverty, political turmoil, and social injustice of all kinds. Destiny even makes the mother wait for eight years to see her first grandchild. Against such a destiny, an individual's odds of winning the struggle are slim indeed. And against such a destiny, the individual has to be strong and enduring so as to survive. However, the Chinese people have survived it, just as they have survived thousands of years of feudalism, in conditions no better than those in the mother's times. This survival is, as Buck seems to suggest, primarily due to mothers: their love of life, their simple but realistic view of life, and their ardent enthusiasm to live life to the fullest under the circumstances. This is a typical quality of the Chinese peasant mother, possibly of mothers of all races.

Buck also painstakingly describes her main character as the epitome of motherhood. Her motherhood, first of all, is displayed in her tenderness:

> Lying like this in the darkness she was filled with tenderness. However impatient she might be in the day, however filled with little sudden angers, at night she was all tenderness—passionate tenderness to the man when he turned to her in need, tender to the children as they lay helpless in sleep, tender to the old woman if she coughed in the night and rising to fetch a little water for her, tender even to the beasts if they stirred and frightened each other with their own stirring. . . . (24)

She also loves children:

There was always something in their [children's] smallness that weakened her heart, and many a time she would pick up a little child, whether of their own house or of some neighbor's, and hold him against her and smell of him hard and fondle him as long as he would bear it, because it was some passionate pleasure to her to feel a little child, although she did not know why. (112)

This love even includes nonhuman lives. She loves young chicks and ducklings in the spring when they come from the shell. When a mother hen forsakes her nest for some reason, she takes the eggs, makes a bag, and slips them against her warm flesh until the young chicks are hatched. She will also faithfully feed the small silkworms, taking great pleasure in watching them grow out of their cocoons, which gives her "satisfaction in her own body" (113).

When there is no real life around her, she takes pleasure in treating nonliving objects as living ones. On a summer day while she is working in the fields, she digs a small waterway to the pond and fetches water from the pond, then pours it into the ditch she has dug. "Over and over she dipped the water and watched the earth grow dark and moist and it seemed to her she fed some thirsting living thing and gave it life" (141).

She loves her husband and apparently enjoys their sex life. But

the man was never enough. In himself he was never enough. She must conceive by him and feel a child take life and shape within her. Then was the act complete and while the child moved and grew she went in a daze of happiness, being fulfilled. (111–12)

Furthermore, she views everyone in the family as her children, even her mother-in-law (30) and her husband (58). Therefore she becomes overbearing with their faults and their sometimes unreasonable wants and needs. All this embodies motherhood in general: its pleasure in giving birth to life, its love of the young, its tenderness toward all loved, and its forgiveness of the needy.

Closely related to the mother's motherhood is her womanhood, her sexual desire. Throughout the novel, the mother is depicted as a woman of "deep heat." Before she is wed, "strange longings" would rise "from within her" (111). After the marriage, she gets to know that she cannot live without her husband:

> That thick, impatient longing in her could even heap itself like thunderous
> clouds into a causeless anger against the man she loved until it resolved
> itself and they clung to each other, and she was satisfied in the old and simple
> way and so was made tranquil again. (111)

Once the man leaves her, her longing for him "came over her like a pain
and her breasts ached when she thought of the thing." Sometimes the pain
becomes so overwhelming that, "Suddenly her longing streamed out of her
like a cry, 'Oh—come home—come home!'" (108).

Then comes the landlord's agent to collect rent. The mother looks at
him: "and there was that great, greedy, starving heart of hers showing in
her own eyes without her knowledge that it did." The man senses her heat
and touched his hand to hers as if by accident. "But the woman felt the
touch and caught its meaning in her blood-like flame" (125). This flame
soon becomes too strong for her to stand:

> Under this man's smooth face and smiling ways, under that gray costly robe
> of his, there was some strange and secret force that poured out of him into
> the shining autumn sun and clung to her and licked about her like a tongue of
> fire. (127)

When the mother meets the agent again during the winter, the agent tries
hard to seduce her by purchasing some silver trinkets for her. The mother is
reluctant yet cooperative, ashamed yet excited. That night, she cannot sleep:
Although her body was cold with the damp chill of the night her cheeks
were burning hot and she could not sleep for a long time and then at last but
lightly. And partly she dreamed of some strange thing shining, and partly
she dreamed of a man's hot hand upon her. (137)

The next summer, when the agent comes back to estimate the crop and
tries to seduce her again, she, though frightened at first, finds out that "such
hunger as was in her now grew raving if it were not fed" (145). Therefore,
she goes to the shrine to meet him, where they have their only sexual encounter.

Among all Buck's women characters, the mother is the one whose sexuality is depicted as the strongest and is made the most explicit. This begs
explanation, and I believe that explanation is not hard to find. As discussed
in chapter 2, women were supposed not to have sexual desire except for the
purpose of fulfilling their men's needs. As a result, in the Chinese literature
of the time, good and virtuous women are often portrayed as devoid of
such desire, and explicit sexuality seems to belong only to those women of

the street. By ascribing such sexuality to the mother, a good and virtuous woman in most aspects, Buck seems to be trying to do women justice, telling her reader that female sexuality is not necessarily an evil thing in and of itself; it is as human as any other aspects of humanity.

However, this explanation, if correct, is only an incomplete one. Buck seems to have two other motivations for depicting the mother's sexuality. First, she informs her reader how sexuality is viewed in Chinese society then and that a woman has to struggle to suppress their sexuality. Second, she treats the mother's sexuality, which is part of her womanhood, as an integral part of her motherhood, thus elevating sexuality to a great height. I will discuss these two in turn.

Although the mother looks forward to and enjoys her encounter with the agent, she does not do it without internal struggle. When she is alone with the agent in the fields, she runs away from him. Before she goes to meet him in the shrine, she suffers the agony of decision making, groaning aloud and crying to her heart: "It could be better if he would not have me—Oh, I wish he would not have me, and that I might be saved" (145). During the sexual encounter, she stops to cover the eyes of the three gods in the shrine with the garment she has laid aside (146). After that, she considers the encounter as "the sweet and evil thing" (146).

Later in her life, her blind daughter dies, her youngest son is executed, and her daughter-in-law seems barren for several years. These are undoubtedly heavy blows for the mother, and she attributes them to her own sins, the greatest of which is what happened on "that hot summer evening" (260, 278, 300). Her assumption is clearly a result of the deeply rooted misconception of female virtue endorsed by society.

We should keep in mind that the mother's sexual encounter with the agent takes place long after the mother is abandoned by her husband. Even so, such an act would be condemned by society, and the woman—never the man—would be doomed as if beyond salvation. The man was free to visit flower houses and to take concubines, but the woman was not supposed to seek other men, even if she is widowed or abandoned. This tradition had been so long and so deeply rooted that even women themselves viewed any encounter with other men than their husbands, alive or dead, as the ultimate sin, a sin that would bring misfortune to the family, a sin that is beyond any means of redemption.

The mother's sexuality, therefore, is both universal and individualized. It is universal in that it is part of womanhood; it is individualized in that it is characteristic of the Chinese context where a woman's sexuality is viewed only as a source of pleasure for man and it should be suppressed if the woman wants it for herself.

About the second possible intention of Buck in portraying the mother as a woman of heat: that sexuality is part of motherhood. To the mother, sexuality and conception are inseparable. When describing how the mother enjoys being with her man in bed, Buck immediately tells us that the reason is not only a sexual one. It is also a means by which the mother can conceive so that her motherhood and her responsibility of perpetuating life can be fulfilled (112). After the husband is gone, the mother's longing for him becomes unbearable:

> Nearly every spring she had given birth, nearly every spring since she was wed, but this spring was her body barren. Once it had seemed a usual common thing to bear a child, and a thing to be done again and again, but now it seemed a joy she had not seen was joy until now, and her loneliness came over her like a pain and her breasts ached when she thought of the thing, and it was this, that she would never bear a child again in such a spring unless her man came home. (108)

She is thinking about her man. She is thinking about childbearing. To her, sexual needs are needs to conceive so as to fulfill her motherhood, and the two are the one and the same.

Heat, to the mother, is the source of warm heart and love of life and the prerequisite for childbearing. Her daughter-in-law is almost flawless in her duties, but is cold in heart. She does not bear children for eight years after being married. The mother firmly believes that all this is because she is slim, pale, and therefore lacking in "heat" (276).

However, no place in the novel is more suggestive of the close relationship between motherhood and womanhood than the following incident: Before her marriage, she meets a young boy, too young to walk, being taken care of by his sister. Holding him in her arms, the mother "smelled of his fat palms and took pleasure in his round cheeks and in his little rosy mouth, and she carried him about with her, setting him astride her sturdy hip. . . ." "Soon without her knowing it this child came to rouse in her a longing she had never known before." It is not only a longing for sons, but "something more, some deep and secret passion for what she did not know" (114).

She then seizes any opportunity to hold the baby boy tightly against her own body, murmuring to and nursing him. When she chews up food and thrusts it into his little mouth from hers, "she laughed, but she did not know why she laughed, for she was not merry, seeing there was such a fierce, deep, painful longing in her which she did not know how to ease" (115).

One day, she is again alone with the boy. He is restless with hunger. "Driven by some dim fierce passion she did not understand but only felt in her blood urging her on," she

> undid her coat and put the child to her own young slender breast and he laid hold on it lustily and sucked hard at it. Then she, standing there staring into his baby face, felt such a tumult in her blood as she had never dreamed of and the tears came into her eyes and sounds rose to her lips, broken sounds that were not words, and she held him strained against her and did not know what it was she felt within herself, full and yearning and passionate, greater than the child, greater than herself. (115)

This incident "roused her as no man had ever done" (113), and "it was an awakening and more almost than marriage. Ever after even the man she wed was most to her because he was a part of motherhood, and not for his own sake only did she love him" (115–16).

It should be clear, even to the most ardent opponents of Freudianism, that this awakening is a combination of motherhood and womanhood. The reader cannot tell one from the other, for the two are one and the same. This is feminine sexuality; this is Chinese motherhood.

However, in the China of that time, only when a woman rightfully belonged to a man did she have womanhood and motherhood. Once her husband has left to seek pleasure for himself, the mother is deprived of her feminine sexuality and motherhood and is faced with humiliation for her reputation. She finds it impossible to tell the truth, since doing so will destroy all her dignity and honor, making it almost impossible to go on with life.

Therefore, she goes to the city and asks a letter writer to forge a letter in the name of her husband, saying that he has a decent job in town, so he cannot come home for spring festival. She also puts in the envelope the paper money she has changed with silver currency, pretending that it was the money sent by him. When the letter arrives and is read by the village's letter writer, the whole village knows that the husband has not deserted her. Thus the rumor of abandonment disappears and the mother regains her dignity, spared of the greatest shame (93–94).

From then on, the mother has a letter forged every year to comfort the grandmother and the children and to deceive the villagers to save her reputation. After her sexual encounter with the agent, however, she thinks it is time for the husband to die. She then goes to the city again to have a letter forged, saying that the man has died in a fire without even leaving any ashes (160–61). The purpose of doing this is to make herself more available to the landlord's agent. However, when she finds him in the city, telling him that "I am widowed," the agent's response is "What is that to me!" (161).

The mother is undoubtedly deceptive and manipulative. But before blaming her, one should consider two facts. First, the mother regrets her lying bitterly ever after. She regards it as one of her two great sins (the other being the sexual encounter with the agent):

> here the sin was, that she had lied and said her man was dead. Almost was it now when she thought of it as if she had put her hand forth and brought his death on him, and she had used this lie of death to hope another man would have her. So all these sins of hers . . . came back fresh and . . . heavier because she could not tell them all but must carry them in herself, and heaviest because she was a woman held in good repute among her fellows. (260)

The second fact concerns the social conditions for women at the time. A woman abandoned was the most ashamed, the most humiliated, and the most degraded. She would have no dignity, honor, or respect left as a result and be thrown to the very bottom of society. Here she is faced with a choice, between lying and being humiliated. She chooses the former, the lesser of the two evils. Put in her shoes, who would have done otherwise?

As this study attempts to show, all Buck's women characters use their limited power to achieve what they deserve. In the mother's case, it means calculation and deception. This by no means suggests that Chinese society condones such acts, but that these women, being deeply oppressed by society, are forced to use whatever resources they have available to gain what little they deserve from life.

Comparing the mother with O-lan, we see differences at first sight: O-lan is inarticulate while the mother is outspoken; O-lan controls her emotions while the mother lets her feelings flow out freely; O-lan helps her husband to achieve prosperity while the mother is abandoned by her man, and O-lan's life is much less stable than the mother's. However, we also see similarities. They are both diligent and responsible; they both possess the ability to endure hardship; they both love life and never lose hope, and they both are ready to sacrifice themselves for their loved ones. While the differences between them result from their differing backgrounds, differing personalities, and differing conditions under which they live, their similarities are suggestive of Buck's deep conviction that Chinese women possess the finest qualities and that they are the mainstay of the society, the driving force of life no matter how hard it is, in spite of the fact that they are among the most oppressed people the world over.

While it is my contention that Buck's mother in The Mother is an embodiment of universal motherhood and at the same time a vividly drawn individual Chinese mother, I do agree with some critics, particularly Doyle (1980), that Buck's characterization is not entirely flawless. In the second half of the novel, when the elder son is married and the mother aged, the mother becomes quite garrulous and even senile. She finds faults with her daughter-in-law, constantly and sometimes unreasonably complains about things, and seems to have lost her mental ability to reason clearly and logically. The sympathy, admiration, and respect she draws from the readers in the first half of the novel lessen considerably in the second half. I see only one explanation for this: Buck simply depicts what she sees would happen to a woman in the mother's situation. According to the Three Obediences, a woman was supposed to obey her eldest son after her husband died, while the son should pay his duty to his parents. In the mother's case, however, when her eldest son marries, she has to give up her bed to the newly wed and takes the pallet behind the curtains, an indication that she has given up her power: "She was lessened in her own eyes from that day on" (209). When her son takes over onto himself all the decision-making for the family, assuming full responsibility as the man of the house, there is nothing the mother can do about it. "Even though she was in name the oldest and the first and mistress over all, she was not first in her own eyes" (209). Therefore, her garrulousness and naggishness, her picking on the daughter-in-law, and her constant complaints are her last desperate effort to maintain some control in the family. Seen in this light, the mother's behavior becomes less unusual and Buck seems less blamable.

Despite all her faults, the mother is still a better portrayed character and with better qualities than her husband. As in the case of Mr. Wu in *Pavilion of Women*, the reader never really gets to know what is in the husband's mind and, after a very brief appearance at the beginning of the novel, he simply vanishes, leaving the reader wondering, together with the mother, why he never sends a word back to explain his departure. However, our brief encounter with him tells us much about him. First, he is vain:

He could set a whole crowd laughing with his songs and wit. . . . When he heard them laugh his heart leaped with pleasure in this power he had, and when he came home again and saw his wife's grave face and sturdy body it seemed to him that only she did not know him for the fine man he truly was, for only she never praised him. (52)

After he forces the mother to make him a new robe,

he put it on and he shined his ring with bits of broken stone and he smoothed his hair with oil he poured from the kitchen bottle and he went swaggering down the street. (62)

Second, the husband is a playboy who hates work and loves pleasure. Unlike the good cousin who is always working on something, he would rather spend his leisure time sleeping and gambling. He never works more than he must, as he thinks: "Why should I wear my good body to the bone to feed them [his family] and never find any merry thing at all for me in my own life?" (51). Instead, "he longed for pleasure and strange sights and any idle joy that he could find in some city far away" (52).

Most importantly, he is not able to see the essence of life. While the mother sees changes in the seemingly monotonous, never-ending life cycle, he sees only monotony:

To him there was no change in time, no hope of any new thing day after day. Even in the coming of the children his wife loved there was no new thing, for to him they were born the same and one was like another and all were to be clothed and fed, and when they were grown they must be wed in their turn and once more children born and all was the same, each day like to another, and there was no new thing. (39)

As if this is not enough, Buck invites us to see the way the husband treats his family. To his wife, he begrudges her even a little break to tend the baby and grows angry "because she stopped so often at her share of the work" (14). He takes it for granted that the mother is to wait on him, never bothering to lift a finger to help her, even though she works in the fields as much as he does. He blames her for bearing children too easily and quickly. He never buys her any jewelry, although he purchases himself a gold ring (which turns out to be a fake). In order to buy a piece of material to make himself a new robe, he takes by force the three silver coins that the mother has brought with her when they were married and has put away for emergency. Despite her protest, he "threw her aside upon the earthen floor . . . and ran out shouting as he ran, 'Cut me off twelve feet of it and the foot and more to spare that is the custom!'" (60).

As for the children, "it was nothing to him that he was the father of sons" (52). He will cuff the children "furiously" if they wake him before his sleep is ended and is seldom merry with them. He will spend money in the teahouse, but begrudges money to buy medicine for his daughter's troubled eyes. He loathes the fact that sometimes the mother puts the children before him (41). To him the children are a burden: "Here I see . . . in my house the same woman and one child after another and all alike weeping and brawling and wanting to be fed" (51).

Buck's intention is thus clear: the mother is the one that loves all, that is responsible for the family, that is ready to sacrifice all she has for her man and children. She is the driving force to push life forward. This power of love, of devotion, and of endurance is perhaps what we recognize in all mothers, making the mother a character with a universal appeal.

As cited previously, some critics hold that the mother is a character lacking in individuality. The reason seems to lie in the fact that the characters in the novel are all anonymous and that the mother's life is uneventful. It is true that no character in the novel is named. When at times characters have to be identified more specifically (There is only one such time), they are referred to as "Li The First" (the husband) and "Li The Third in the last generation" (the husband's father)(79). However, this does not necessarily prevent the character from being individualized. It is another indication that Buck knows her characters well, as such a means of address is common in rural China.

Second, it is also true that the mother's life is less eventful than the life of the women characters in Buck's other novels. Compared to O-lan in *The Good Earth*, for example, the mother's life has fewer dramatic ups and downs. The mother's family is poor, but its life is rather stable throughout: there is no famine, no starvation, no leaving home for far-off places, and no fear of robbers and bandits, although there is death and birth. But again this serves Buck's purpose well, for she intends to create a universal, ordinary mother character, and ordinary mothers do not always have dramatic lives. They struggle with daily routines, with everyday necessities, with deaths of their elders, and with births, upbringing, and marriages of their children. To them, these events are significant. And it is through these seemingly ordinary events that we see motherhood. The lack of drama in the mother's life is therefore a deliberate effort by the novelist: In order to create an image of universal mother, Buck needed a typical mother to embody motherhood of all societies.

Moreover, in portraying the universal mother in these most ordinary events, Buck never loses her sight in treating her as an individual. As we have seen, Buck displays the mother's individuality in her deep love for and ardent struggle in life, in her admirable power of endurance, in her unique womanhood that is inseparable from her motherhood, and in her deceptive acts to save her honor and dignity. All these qualities are there for the careful reader to discover and to appreciate.

Thus, *The Mother* seems like a Chinese painting. Against a uniquely Chinese landscape, we see, at a distance, human figures that are representative of their types. If there is a shepherd, we might think that he can be a shepherd of all races. However, only when we step forward toward the painting, examining it more closely, do we see the unique shape of his eyes, the unique size of his nose, the unique density of his beard, the unique style of his pipe, and the unique make of his whip he uses to direct his sheep, all exquisitely drawn, all carefully crafted. The mother is such a shepherd in Buck's painting, a representative of all mothers and a unique individual at the same time.

6

Conclusion

Uᴺᴛɪʟ ɴᴏᴡ, ɪ ʜᴀᴠᴇ ᴀɴᴀʟʏᴢᴇᴅ ᴛʜᴇ ᴡᴏᴍᴇɴ ᴄʜᴀʀᴀᴄᴛᴇʀs ɪɴ ꜰɪᴠᴇ ᴏꜰ ʙᴜᴄᴋ'ꜱ Chinese novels, concentrating on their typicality and individualization and their utilization of the limited power grudgingly granted them by society to fight for what they deserve.

Although opposing each other, typicality and individualization are closely related concepts. If a character is totally typical, predictable in every way according to her type, she will be a flat character lacking in literary merits. If, on the other hand, a character is individualized without being in any way typical, with no predictable traits and deeds, she will lose credibility and the characterization will not be a success either. Therefore, a successful characterization is that which combines the two. It is my contention that Buck's major characters are such combinations of typicality and individualization,[1] testifying to her dexterity in characterization.

The characters in the five novels are individualized to various degrees. On the typicality–individualization continuum, Madame Wu, in *Pavilion of Women*, is the most individualized; O-lan, in *The Good Earth*, is the next most individualized; Peony, the bondmaid in *Peony* and Kwei-lan, in *East Wind: West Wind*, are more typical than individualized; and, finally, the anonymous mother in *The Mother* is the least individualized. Schematically, this can be presented as follows:

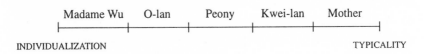

Throughout the book, I have been arguing that characterization, however important it might be in literary analysis, should not be studied in isolation. Rather, it should be examined in relation to the themes of the

121

work in question. Therefore, the different degrees of individualization of these characters are seen to have resulted from the differing themes of the novels in which they appear.

There is another important reason for the typicality of Buck's characters. Because her readers were mostly Westerners, Buck needed typicality in her characters to help the readers to understand the cultural context in which individual characters function. As a result, Buck's characters will come to the reader as being typical at first, but will gradually become individualized as the story moves forward. The combination of typicality and individualization works well both in laying a solid foundation for Western readers to interpret the characters' behaviors and in bringing the characters alive as real human beings, each facing different conflicts, in a variety of social, familial situations.

In *Pavilion of Women*, Buck creates a highly individualized Madame Wu because she intends to inform her Western readers that Chinese women can be both beautiful and intelligent, both practical and philosophical, both tender and strong. They yearn for freedom and are capable of achieving it. They have the ability to love everyone. The combination of all these characteristics helps break the stereotypical images of Chinese women in particular and women of all races in general. In other words, the individualization of Madame Wu is essential for Buck to destroy stereotypes, thus fitting well with the theme of the novel.

Similarly, because the theme of *The Good Earth* is the ups and downs of a Chinese peasant and the close relationship between the Chinese peasants and the land, it calls for individualized rather than typical characters. With her quietness and inarticulateness, her endurance of hardship, her keen perception of life, her courage to do whatever it takes to help the family survive, and her unique contribution to Wang Lung's rise to prosperity, O-lan the individualized character helps to bring out the theme in this epic of Chinese peasant life.

In *Peony*, Buck intends to show the attitudes of Chinese people toward a different race. Therefore, she depicts the life of a typical bondmaid in a Jewish family. The typicality of Peony is needed because she is meant to be a representative of servants so that the reader will understand the oppression they face. She is also a representative of the Chinese people, whose values of social interaction are characterized by warmth and care, values that a Westerner may find imposing.

East Wind: West Wind is about how the Chinese people adapt to a changing time. Through Kwei-lan, again a rather typical character, although with her unique individual characteristics, Buck was able to demonstrate convincingly that the Chinese people are capable of surviving the conflict between the two cultures although such an adaptation is forced rather than self-motivated. Moreover, through Kwei-lan's final triumph, particularly the birth of her first male child, which is the result of her change and at the same time a fulfillment of the highest duty of a traditional Chinese wife, Buck indicat es that when two cultures come into conflict, the ideal resolution is the union of both rather than the complete disappearance of one.

Lastly, the mother in *The Mother* seems more typical than individualized because Buck's intention is to create a universal mother. A motherhood of universality, by definition, should embody characteristics of mothers of all races. By depicting a rather typical mother, Buck succeeds in her intention, showing that the Chinese mother is no different from the mother on a Nebraska farm, in an African village, or in a coastal city in the Mediterranean. If the mother were as individualized as Madame Wu, Buck would not have succeeded in bringing out this fundamental similarity in motherhood and, accordingly, in humanity.

I have also shown that all of Buck's women characters use their limited power to achieve what they deserve, although each one of them has her own ways of doing so. This reveals the social conditions under which Chinese women during Buck's times lived. Treated as no more than sex objects for men, instruments to perpetuate the family name, and laborers within the confinement of home, Chinese women were deprived of many basic rights and had very little power in the familial arena. However, they were human beings after all, and they had, just as their male counterparts, the desire to love, to be happy, to be respected, and to maintain honor, dignity, and self-esteem. Because society did not provide them the necessary recourse to do all this, they had to resort to underground means, even if they would appear a little sagacious, a little deceptive. This does not suggest that Buck's women are dishonest. They are always aware that they are doing things in the gray area between right and wrong, or, occasionally, outright wrong, and they very often bitterly regret afterward. On the contrary, these deeds are an indication of the intelligence of these characters: they are able to thread their way through a maze of behavior codes, stated or unstated, and maneuver within the boundaries of Confucianism for the sake of others as well as for their own.

With their different degrees of individuality and typicality, Buck's women characters, taken together, provide the reader with a realistic picture of Chinese women. This is seen also in Buck's detailed descriptions of the life of her characters and the dialogues among them. While this lies outside the scope of this book, it is not difficult to see how the Confucian doctrines and the social conditions concerning Chinese women, discussed in chapter 2, are truthfully reflected in the novels herein analyzed.

Because of her knowledge of China and her love of the Chinese people, coupled with her highly acclaimed creative skills, Buck has artistically and faithfully presented the Chinese people to the world. By so doing, Buck contributed a great deal to destroying the stereotypes of the Chinese people, particularly Chinese women. Her women characters, as we have seen, are nothing like the way they have been perceived by society, as summarized by Margery Wolf (1985):

> Women were narrow-hearted. They were incapable of understanding the finer points of human relations on which all civilized life depended. They gossiped and were jealous and quarrelsome, scolding other members of the family and even the neighbors when aroused. They were dependent, timid, and prone to weeping. They were ignorant and stupid and irresponsible. Worst yet, women were dangerous. Their menstrual secretions, if handled improperly, could cause men to sicken, gods to turn away in disgust, and families to decline in poverty. Their sexuality could drain men of their strength or drive them insane with lust. According to some they were sexually insatiable; according to others, they were frigid. In elite families they were expected to (and sometimes did) defend their chastity from even a suspicion of stain, with their lives if necessary, but they were considered morally and physically weak. (2)

Lastly, Buck seems to have been an ardent feminist. Although she never claimed such a position, her feminist views are not difficult to find in her works. As such critics as Doan and Doyle, among others, have pointed out that Buck's women characters possess better qualities and are better crafted than male characters. This study has yielded evidence for this observation. For example, in *The Mother*, the mother cares and provides for the family while her husband deserts her and the family for his own pleasure. In *Pavilion of Women*, Madame Wu runs everything in the house and pursues spiritual freedom and internal peace while her husband, portrayed as weak, selfish, and unintelligent, spends most of his time in flower houses, satisfied only in physical pleasure. In *The Good Earth*, it is O-lan who, at critical times, saves the family and enables it to be prosperous, but her husband, Wang Lung, becomes selfish and vain and takes concubines home. While the society views women as weak, less intelligent, and less capable, Buck depicts women as strong, more intelligent and more capable. This seeming prejudice against men, as I alluded to when analyzing *Pavilion of Women* in chapter 3, might have been a deliberate effort by Buck to go over the limit to correct something that has been wrong for too long.

There is other evidence for considering Buck a feminist. In her works, both fiction and nonfiction (*Of Men and Women* [1941] for instance), her comments on feminist issues are abundant, and she speaks of women's conditions with sympathy, of their qualities with admiration, and of their triumphs with joy. She sees things through a woman's eyes and values women's experience. When describing Chiuming's having to sell her flesh for a roof to live under, for example, Buck speaks of it with indignation, protesting it openly through her character's subdued voice.

Being a feminist might be acceptable nowadays, but it took conscious-ness, perceptiveness, a loving heart for the oppressed gender, and the cour-age to speak for them to be one in Buck's times. Were Buck living now, there is little doubt that she would be a most ardent and discerning sup-porter of the feminist movement.

With her skill and success in characterization, and in other aspects such as setting, plot, and style, Buck the writer deserves more attention than what she has hitherto received. To ignore her, as we have done for decades, is to ignore women, who hold up "half the sky," and to ignore the Chinese people, who comprise more than a quarter of the human race.

Notes

Chapter 1: Introduction

1. However, Doyle (1980, 153) thinks that Buck has produced too much. He points out that since writing had become an obsession for her, she did not think out, polish, and revise many of her novels as she should have, especially those written in her post–Nobel Prize era.

2. The lack of attention Buck receives aroused certain indignation from those critics who think highly of her. Harris (1969, 361–62) records that in the late sixties, Dr. Kyung Cho Chung, a renowned Korean writer, wrote the following:

> Although our only woman Nobel Prize winner for literature is excluded from the absurd recently publicized White House Library list, her works are not excluded from book stores, shelves and tables in the homes of countless readers. She is very much alive, and unwearyingly prolific, giving us now her finest novels of her primary literary domain, Eastern Asia. It is hoped that many in the White House will read it [*The Living Reed*] to better understand not only Korea, but also other newly independent Asian countries which present a challenge to the United Nations, as well as the United States.

3. Under this pseudonym, Buck published five novels: *The Townsman* (1945), *The Angry Wife* (1947), *The Long Love* (1949), *Bright Procession* (1952), and *Voices in the House* (1953).

4. In his revised edition of *Pearl S. Buck*, Doyle (1980: 83) notes a third factor that contributes to Buck's works being neglected, specifically concerning Buck's *The Good Earth*: "the critics did not first discover *The Good Earth* and then spread its reputation until it was picked up by the general public." Therefore, "the critics were offended because the public had, so to speak, stolen a march on them."

Chapter 3: Aristocratic Women

1. In fact, a Chinese man does not find freedom easy to obtain either. When Fengmo is talking with his American girlfriend, he finds out that he cannot send Linyi away and marry the American girl, because he realizes that "he was not free. The hands of his ancestors were fastened on him, and the hands of his sons and grandsons not yet born beckoned on him." He tells the girl:

I know that I am made, not only by heaven, but also by my family whose roots are in legend, and I cannot live for myself alone. . . . If I were to give [you] my body, which is not mine, I should be robbing the generations. (296)

Chapter 4: Servant Women in *Peony*

1.   These conquests themselves were not of a racial nature. They were political.

2.   This does not suggest that there are no racial distinctions in present China. In fact, besides the Han, there are some fifty-six peoples in that country who have kept their traditions and identity.

Chapter 5: Peasant Women

1.   Perhaps it is due to this fact that the previous critics all ignored the mother's sexuality and believed that it was only her desire for childbearing that drove her to have sex with the agent.

Chapter 6: Conclusion

1.   This does not mean that every character should be such. At times a writer might deliberately create typical minor characters so as to make the main characters stand out more sharply. Kwei-lan's father's three concubines (*East Wind: West Wind*) and Madame Wu's mother-in-law (*Pavilion of Women*) belong to this group.

Bibliography

Adams, J. Donald. 1934. "A True Epitome of Motherhood: Mrs. Buck's Deeply Elemental Novel of Chinese Peasant Life." *New York Times* (14 January): 1, 18.

———. 1944. *The Shape of Books to Come.* New York: Viking.

A. C. 1930. "Review on *East Wind: West Wind.*" *Boston Transcript* (3 May): 8.

Ayscough, Florence. 1931. "The Real China." Review of *The Good Earth,* by Pearl S. Buck. *Saturday Review of Literature* 7 (21 March): 676.

Baym, Nina. 1981. "Melodramas of Beset Manhood: How Theories of American Fiction Exclude Women Authors." *American Quarterly* 33: 123–39.

Bentley, Phyllis. 1935. "The Art of Pearl S. Buck." *English Journal* (December): 791–800.

Bitker, M. M. 1961. "Window on Several Worlds." *Saturday Review* (October): 41.

Brickell, Herschel. 1934. Review of *The Mother,* by Pearl S. Buck. *New York Evening Post* (20 January): 7.

Brown, Catherine. 1948. "China: A Time and Place of Tolerance." Review of *Peony,* by Pearl S. Buck. *Saturday Review of Literature* 31 (May): 23.

Buck, Pearl S. 1930. *East Wind: West Wind.* New York: John Day.

———. 1931. "Chinese Women." *Pacific Affairs* (October): 905–9.

———. 1932a. *East and West and the Novel: Sources of Early Chinese Novels.* Peking: College of Chinese Studies.

———. 1932b. *The Good Earth.* New York: John Day.

———. 1932c. "The Old Chinese Nurse." *The Country Gentleman* (June): 14–15, 36.

———. 1933a. "Mrs. Buck Replies to Her Chinese Critic." *New York Times* (15 January): 2, 17.

———. 1933b. "On the Writing of Novels." *Randolph-Macon Woman's College Bulletin* (June): 3–10.

———. 1934. *The Mother.* New York: John Day.

———. 1939. *The Chinese Novel.* New York: John Day.

———. 1941. *Of Men and Women.* New York: John Day.

———. 1946. *Pavilion of Women.* New York: John Day.

———. 1948a. "Pearl S. Buck Talks about *Peony.*" Dustjacket, *Peony.* New York: John Day.

———. 1948b. *Peony.* New York: John Day.

———. 1954. *My Several Worlds.* New York: John Day.

———. 1958. *American Triptych*. New York: John Day.

———. 1972. *China Past and Present*. New York: John Day.

Buck, Pearl S. and Carlos Romulo. 1958. *Friend to Friend*. New York: Day.

Butcher, Fanny. 1934. Review of *The Mother,* by Pearl S. Buck. *Chicago Daily Tribune* (13 January): 15.

Canfield, Dorothy. 1932. Review of *Sons*. *Book-of-the-Month Club News*.

Carson, E. H. A. 1939. "Pearl Buck's Chinese." *Canadian Bookman* (June): 55–59.

"Chinese Life." 1930. Review of *East Wind: West Wind,* by Pearl S. Buck. *New York Times* (April): 8.

Conn, Peter. 1996. *Pearl S. Buck: A Cultural Biography*. New York: Cambridge University Press.

Doan, Caoly. 1965. *Image of the Chinese Family in Pearl Buck's Novels*. Ph.D. diss., St. John's University, Brooklyn, N.Y.

Doyle, Paul. 1980. *Pearl S. Buck*. Rev. ed. *Twayne's United States Authors Series, 85*. New York: Twayne.

E. G. 1930. Review of *East Wind: West Wind,* by Pearl S. Buck. *Pacific Affairs* 3: 506.

Forbes, H. R. 1948. Review of *Peony,* by Pearl S. Buck. *Library Journal* 73 (April): 651.

Fuson, Ben. 1952. *Which Text Shall I Choose for American Literature? A Descriptive and Statistical Comparison of Currently Available Survey Anthologies and Reprint Series in American Literature*. Parkville, Mo.: Park College Press.

Garnett, David. 1934. Review of *The Mother*, by Pearl S. Buck. *The New Statesman and Nation* 7 (27 January): 120.

Gray, James. 1946. *On Second Thought*. Minneapolis: University of Minnesota Press.

Gu, Yueguo. 1990. "Politeness Phenomena in Modern Chinese." *Journal of Pragmatics* 14: 237–57.

Harris, Theodore F. 1969. *Pearl S. Buck: A Biography*. New York: John Day.

Hayford, Charles W. 1992. "*The Good Earth*, Revolution, and the American RAJ in China." Paper presented at Pearl S. Buck Centennial Symposium at Randolph-Macon Woman's College, Lynchburg, Virginia.

Henchoz, Ami. 1943. "A Permanent Element in Pearl Buck's Novels." *English Studies* (August): 97–103.

Hutchinson, Paul. 1931. "Breeder of Life." Review of *The Good Earth,* by Pearl S. Buck. *Christian Century* 48 (20 May): 683.

Kang, Younghill. 1931. "Controversial Article on *The Good Earth*." *New Republic* (1 July): 185.

Kiang, Kang–Hu. 1933. "A Chinese Scholar's View of Mrs. Buck's Novel." *New York Times* (15 January): 2, 16.

Kristeva, Julia. 1974. *About Chinese Women*. New York: Urizen Books.

Lauter, Paul. 1983. "Race and Gender in the Shaping of the American Literary Canon: A Case Study from the Twenties." *Feminist Studies* 9, no. 3: 436–63.

LeBar, Barbara. 1988. "The Subject Is Marriage." *Journal of Evolutionary Psychology* 9, nos. 3–4: 264–69.

Li Bo, B. A. 1989. *The Chinese as Portrayed in the Writings of Several Prominent American Authors*. Master's thesis, Stephen F. Austin State University, Nacogdoches, Texas.

Lin, Yutang. 1935. *My Country and My People*. New York: John Day Company.

Lipscomb, Elizabeth J., Frances E. Webb, and Peter Conn, eds. 1994. *The Several Worlds of Pearl S. Buck: Essays Presented at a Centennial Symposium, Randolph-Macon Woman's College, March 26–28, 1992*. Westport, Conn.: Greenwood Press.

Overton, Jeanne K. 1942. *Pearl Buck: Bibliography of Criticism*. Boston: Simmons College.

"Pearl S. Buck's *Peony*." 1948. Dustjacket, *Peony*. New York: John Day.

Peffer, Nathaniel. 1930. Review of *East Wind: West Wind*, by Pearl S. Buck. *Books* (18 May): 6.

Rabb, Jane M. 1992. "Who's Afraid of Pearl S. Buck?" *Randolph-Macon Woman's College Bulletin* (Fall): 6–7.

Review of *East Wind: West Wind*, by Pearl S. Buck. 1948. *Springfield Republican* (30 May): 10b.

Review of *The Good Earth*, by Pearl S. Buck. 1931. *New Statesman and Nation* 1 (16 May): 430.

Review of *Peony*, by Pearl S. Buck. 1948. *New Yorker* 24 (15 May): 121.

Richards, G. R. B. 1934. Review of *The Mother*, by Pearl S. Buck. *Boston Transcript* (13 January): 1.

Ross, Mary. 1934. "A Nameless Mother on the Good Earth." Review of *The Mother*, by Pearl S. Buck. *Books* (14 January): 3.

———. 1948. "House of the Bondmaid." *New York Herald Tribune Weekly Book Review* (9 May): 17.

Schneider, Isidore. 1930. Review of *East Wind: West Wind*, by Pearl S. Buck. *New Republic* 63 (May): 24.

———. 1934. "Mrs. Buck's New Novel." Review of *The Mother*, by Pearl S. Buck. *New Republic* 78 (14 March): 136.

Scoggin, M. C. 1948. Review of *Peony*, by Pearl S. Buck. *Horn Book* 24 (July): 290.

Seaver, Edwin. 1930. "Review of *East Wind: West Wind*." *New York Evening Post* (12 April): 10m.

Spiller, Robert, Willard Thorp, Thomas H. Johnson, and Henry Seidel Canby. 1948. *Literary History of the United States*. New York: Macmillan.

Stone, Geoffrey. 1934. Review of *The Mother*, by Pearl S. Buck. *Commonweal* 19 (9 March): 528.

Van Doren, Carl. 1940. *The American Novel 1789–1939*. New York: Macmillan.

Van Doren, Mark. 1934. "Abstract Woman." Review of *The Mother*, by Pearl S. Buck. *The Nation* 138 (17 January): 78.

Van Gulik, Robert Hans. 1971. *La vie sexuelle dans la Chine ancienne*. Gallimard.

Voiles, Jane. 1948. Review of *Peony*, by Pearl S. Buck. *San Francisco Chronicle* (10 May): 18.

Witke, Roxane. 1973. "Women as Politician in China of the 1920s." In *Women in China.*, edited by Marilyn B. Young. Ann Arbor: Center for Chinese Studies, University of Michigan.

Wolf, Margery. 1985. *Revolution Postponed: Women in Contemporary China*. Stanford, Calif.: Stanford University Press.

Yu, Yuh–chao. 1988. "Chinese influence on Pearl S. Buck." *Tamkang Review: A Quarterly of Comparative Studies between Chinese and Foreign Literatures* 11, no. 1: 23–41.

Index

aristocratic women, 43, 44
arranged marriage, 42
Asian critics, 17

Biographies of Virtuous Women, 33
bondmaids, 81, 83, 84, 88
Book of Changes, 18, 30
Book of Han Dynasty (Han Shu), 32
Book of Poems, 30
Book of Rites, 31
bourgeois revolution, 34
Buck, John Lossing , 24
Buck, Pearl S.: American novels, 16; Chinese background, 28; Chinese education, 24; Chinese novels, 16, 121; language, 20; literary achievements, 20; novels, 9, 11, 16, 22, 36, 78, 107, 108; productivity, 12; works, 10–17, 19, 21–23, 79, 127
Buddhist, 24, 75

characterization, 9–10, 17, 20–23, 26–27, 43, 47, 51, 58, 75, 78, 81, 87–90, 117, 121, 125
Chinese: characters, 22, 23; civilization, 81, 89; critics, 12, 18, 19; culture, 24, 59, 80, 87; customs, 22, 95; government, 12, 13; history 24; language, 30, 35, 38; life 12–13, 16–18, 19, 25; literature, 42, 112; men, 22; novel, 12, 15, 25–26, 40–41; peasants, 24 103, 122; people, 10, 17, 46, 49–50, 58, 78–80, 88, 93, 96, 122–24; scholars, 16–17, 30; society, 16, 34, 35, 50, 69, 84, 97, 113, 116
Chinese novels: *The Dream of the Red Mansion, 40, 41, 83; Family, 40, 41, 130; Shui Hu Zhuan (All Men Are Brothers), 12, 19*

Chinese women, 9–11, 22–23, 35, 43–46, 49, 52, 58, 59, 74–76, 85, 88, 91, 96, 106, 116, 122–24
Communists, 12–13
concubine, 39–42, 56, 60, 62–65, 70, 76, 87, 92, 104
Confucianism, 30–31, 33–34, 40–41, 123; Confucian classics, 38; Confucian modal, 104; Confucian scholars, 32; doctrines, 33, 74, 75, 124; ethics, 24; moral codes, 41, 48, 52, 55, 65; morality, 57; practice, 38; standards, 48, 52, 54
Confucian teacher, 83
Confucius, 5, 28, 30–31, 33, 37
Conrad, Joseph 27
continuum, 10, 58, 88, 121
Cuckoo, 98, 104–5

divorce, 34, 35, 39, 42. See also *lihun*
dynasties: Han dynasty, 31, 32; Ming dynasty, 33; Qing dynasty, 30, 80; Song dynasty, 32, 36; Tang dynasty, 36; Yuan dynasty, 80

East Wind, West Wind: Pearl S. Buck, The Woman Who Embraced the World (film), 15
East Wind: West Wind, 39, 41, 44, 45, 58, 75, 79
educated women, 9, 38, 46, 53, 72, 105
Exile, The, 11

Faulkner, William, 27
female equality, 34
female virtue, 31, 113
feminist, 103, 124; movement, 125
First Lady, 47, 54, 60, 66, 74
Flaubert, Gustav 27